"A brief overview and helpful introduction to what is probably Kierkegaard's most read and most puzzling text. It wisely locates this telling of the Abraham story within Kierekgaard's larger 'attack upon Christendom,' his critique of the Danish church for making faith too easy and the closely related Hegelian philosophy for making faith too 'reasonable.' It nicely specifies the distinctive way in which biblical faith is 'absurd' or 'paradoxical.'"

—MEROLD WESTPHAL

Distinguished Professor of Philosophy Emeritus, Fordham University

"As a Kierkegaard scholar, I am all too aware that many students first encounter Kierkegaard through *Fear and Trembling*, a pseudonymous text that is not only difficult to read but disquieting in its conclusions. What distinguishes Paul Martens' new commentary on *Fear and Trembling* is that it confronts these challenges head-on, while never forgetting that Kierkegaard's masterwork is meant to be provocative, perhaps even (as Kierkegaard himself put it) 'terrifying.'"

—CHRISTOPHER B. BARNETT

Associate Professor, Department of Theology & Religious Studies,
Villanova University

READING KIERKEGAARD I

CASCADE COMPANIONS

The Christian theological tradition provides an embarrassment of riches: from Scripture to modern scholarship, we are blessed with a vast and complex theological inheritance. And yet this feast of traditional riches is too frequently inaccessible to the general reader.

The Cascade Companions series addresses the challenge by publishing books that combine academic rigor with broad appeal and readability. They aim to introduce nonspecialist readers to that vital storehouse of authors, documents, themes, histories, arguments, and movements that comprise this heritage with brief yet compelling volumes.

TITLES IN THIS SERIES:

READING KIERKEGAARD I

Fear and Trembling

PAUL MARTENS

CASCADE *Books* • Eugene, Oregon

READING KIERKEGAARD I
Fear and Trembling

Cascade Companions 31

Cascade Books
An Imprint of Wipf and Stock Publishers
199 W. 8th Ave., Suite 3
Eugene, OR 97401

www.wipfandstock.com

PAPERBACK ISBN: 978-1-62032-019-8
HARDCOVER ISBN: 978-1-4982-8710-4
EBOOK ISBN: 978-1-5326-1357-9

Cataloguing-in-Publication data:

Names: Martens, Paul Henry.
Title: Reading Kierkegaard I : Fear and Trembling / Paul Martens.
Description: Eugene, OR : Cascade Books, 2017 | Series: Cascade Companions 31 | Includes bibliographical references and index.
Identifiers: ISBN 978-1-62032-019-8 (paperback) | ISBN 978-1-4982-8710-4 (hardcover) | ISBN 978-1-5326-1357-9 (ebook)
Subjects: LCSH: Kierkegaard, Søren, 1813–1855. Frygt og bæven. | Christianity—Philosophy.
Classification: B4373.F793 M37 2017 (paperback) | B4373.F793 M37 (ebook)

Manufactured in the U.S.A.   01/19/17

To Alan

CONTENTS

PREFACE

READING SØREN KIERKEGAARD IS a task that requires a relatively high level of intellectual investment. It is only fair that I make this statement up front. Further, reading Kierkegaard rightly also requires a relatively high level of vulnerability. In my experience, vulnerability is often more difficult to render than intellectual investment. For those willing to risk their preconceived understandings of Christianity (along with the requisite time and energy) in order to sit patiently with Kierkegaard, however, all I can promise is that Kierkegaard will continue to walk alongside you—sometimes exhorting, sometimes encouraging—for the rest of your life.

Kierkegaard is difficult to read today because he wrote in a particular time in a particular location using the particular literary tools and language of his era. In short, he wrote for a well-educated, mid-nineteenth-century readership located primarily in Copenhagen, Denmark. In doing so, he often employed various literary conventions borrowed from the Romantics* and language and categories heavily indebted to ancient and modern philosophy (and especially Hegel*).

That said, Kierkegaard continues to speak to us today because his self-confessed task is the task that must be articulated anew for each generation: to become a Christian. In his context, he understood that his task was to "introduce

Christianity into Christendom."[1] As he outlined in his posthumously published *The Point of View*, this task gave his authorship a loose unity with a particular shape and direction.[2] Generally speaking, Kierkegaard's early writings were published pseudonymously for the purpose of drawing his readers from the aesthetic* and from the speculative* to a direct encounter with God; his later writings were published under his own name for the purpose of leading Christians to a deeper understanding of what is essential to Christianity, that is, what encountering God entails for one's everyday existence.[3] Sometimes, therefore, he speaks sharply and polemically; sometimes he speaks softly and sympathetically. Throughout, he seeks to speak indirectly, to function as a midwife that helps with the birth of Christianity and then disappears. Why? Kierkegaard argues that he must disappear because either one becomes a Christian individually before God or one simply does not become a Christian.

The two texts that constitute this *Reading Kierkegaard* miniseries—*Fear and Trembling* (1843) and *Works of Love* (1847)—were published a mere four years apart. However, they are worlds apart in terms of style and substance: the

1. Kierkegaard, *Journals and Papers,* VI 6317. In this and all future references to Kierkegaard's *Journals and Papers*, the first (Roman) number refers to the volume number, followed by the specific entry number (and not page number).

2. It might be best to understand Kierkegaard's *Point of View* in the same vein as Augustine's *Confessions*, that is, as a highly stylized attempt to contextualize one's life within the work of God (or, in Kierkegaard's case, Governance). See, for example, Rae, *Kierkegaard and Theology*, 5–34.

3. Although these statements are generally true, the arrangement of his authorship is a little more complex than intimated here. For a list of his publications and their "authors," see the Appendix. For a basic account of his authorship, see Kierkegaard, *The Point of View*, and Evans, *Kierkegaard: An Introduction*, 24–45.

first is a "dialectical lyric" published under the pseudonym Johannes *de silentio*; the second is a collection of "Christian deliberations" published under Kierkegaard's own name. Yet, they have the same overarching *telos*. In order to justify the choice of these divergent texts as the means to grasp what Kierkegaard is on about as an author, I defer to Kierkegaard's own words that were penned in his journal years before either of these texts was written: "Fear and trembling (see Philippians 2:12) is not the *primus motor* in the Christian life, for it is love; but it is what the oscillating *balance wheel* is to the clock—it is the oscillating *balance wheel* of the Christian life."[4] It is my hope that these two volumes preliminarily and provocatively illuminate how Kierkegaard's complex and difficult authorship seeks to serve his reader in the daily struggle of Christian life.

Of course, there are other very good introductions to *Fear and Trembling* available to the interested reader, especially John Lippitt's *Routledge Philosophy Guidebook to Kierkegaard and Fear and Trembling* and Claire Carlisle's *Kierkegaard's Fear and Trembling*. This volume is not an attempt to repeat the strengths of those volumes, most notably Lippitt's extensive engagement with the secondary literature and Carlisle's thorough expository retracing of the text itself. Rather, the specific purposes of this succinct volume are (1) to illuminate the internal logic of the text in a manner that renders the text more accessible; (2) to highlight the links between *Fear and Trembling* and Kierkegaard's broader context in a way that helps one make sense of some of its more opaque sections; and (3) to attend to the theological themes that permeate and drive the text. Concentrating on these elements, therefore, complements the exceptional work that has already been done by

4. Kierkegaard, *Journals and Papers*, III 2383.

others who, like me, have spent many years grappling with Kierkegaard's indomitable *Fear and Trembling*.

Speaking autobiographically, my own debts to Kierkegaard continue to accrue at an alarming rate as I repeatedly become aware of what I have learned through him (often without recognizing it until much later). Kierkegaard regarded his authorship as his own education, of sorts, as an account of his own need for "upbringing and development."[5] I dare say that something similar has happened to me, even if only in a partial and slightly equivocal sense. Many have walked alongside and helped me tremendously in this journey—Jerry McKenny, Phil Quinn, Cyril O'Regan, Ralph McInerny, Steve Evans, Bob Roberts, Lee Barrett, Bob Perkins, Sylvia Walsh, Gordon Marino, Cynthia Lund, and Jon Stewart have all served as wise guides in one way or another (and my frequent failure to follow is certainly not due to a lack on their part); Will Williams, Dan Marrs, KC Flynn, Ian Panth, David Cramer, Mark Morton, Randy Blythe, Willie Adler, John Campbell, Chris Adler, and the students who suffered through my graduate seminar on Kierkegaard's late authorship have all served as thoughtful and generous reading companions; Laura Lysen, Malcolm Foley, Cody Strecker, Joao Chaves, Brandon Morgan, Bradley Varnell, Nicholas Krause, and Tyler Davis have all read a significant portion of this manuscript with care, and I have no way to acknowledge adequately the collective insight they have contributed; finally, I want to single out Tom Millay because he has indispensably contributed to the strength of this volume in manifold ways. Each of these gracious individuals has demonstrated that loving the neighbor is, in fact, compatible with reading Kierkegaard, and for that I am most grateful.

5. Kierkegaard, *Point of View*, 12.

I also want to thank Charlie Collier for continuing to believe in me, and more importantly, for believing that reading Kierkegaard is still important enough to warrant the publication of these volumes. With tremendous respect and gratitude for all of these generous friends and colleagues, I also want to note that my "Kierkegaardian education" started two decades ago when I read him for the first time in a graduate class taught by Alan Torrance. For that providential moment in my life (and several since), I will always be indebted to Alan. In a small gesture of gratitude, I dedicate this book to him.

All Saints' Eve

2015

PRELIMINARY NOTES ON THE TEXT

BECAUSE READING *FEAR AND Trembling* entails its own difficulties, I want to be entirely clear up front about a few things. First, in this volume, direct quotations will be drawn from the recent translation of *Fear and Trembling* by Sylvia Walsh (coedited by C. Stephen Evans and Sylvia Walsh) because (1) it is eminently readable, (2) it contains judicious footnotes for help with obscure references in the text, and (3) it contains excellent introductory material for the novice reader. That said, in all references to *Fear and Trembling*, page numbers (*a*) will be provided in the text itself, and (*b*) will correspond to the Walsh translation—and additionally, because of its continued prevalence, to the translation by Howard V. Hong and Edna H. Hong published by Princeton University Press in 1983 (which also contains *Repetition*). Page references will therefore appear, for example, as (33/38), where the first number refers to the pagination of the Walsh translation and the second refers to the Hong and Hong translation.

Second, the chapters of this text match the discrete sections identified within *Fear and Trembling. Fear and Trembling* is rather idiosyncratic in that it is not a book constructed out of chapters in the manner we are familiar with (though, throughout the course of this volume, I have given in to the temptation to refer to them as "chapters").

Nonetheless, I have attempted to follow the logic of the divisions in Kierkegaard's text and, for this reason, the chapters in this volume are rather asymmetric.

Third, because this volume is written for an audience that may not yet be familiar with Kierkegaard's corpus or its philosophical, literary, and theological context or referents, I have provided a glossary at the end of this volume that attempts to define or describe select important terms. These terms are marked with an asterisk (*) the first time they appear in the text.

Fourth, because this volume ought to serve as merely an entrée into the world of reading Kierkegaard, I have provided a very short list of recommended readings for further exploration at the end of the text (preceding the Bibliography). This list is by no means definitive or exhaustive. Rather, it should be understood as an attempt to make it easier to continue to explore the depth of (*a*) the individual chapters and *Fear and Trembling* as a whole and also (*b*) Kierkegaard's corpus and the recurring themes that exercise him (and many other theologians and philosophers as well).

Lastly, all direct biblical quotations, except when included in portions of text from Kierkegaard's writings, are from the NRSV.

INTRODUCTION

SØREN AABYE KIERKEGAARD (1813–55) was born in Copenhagen, Denmark, and he lived in the city for virtually his entire life. His father, Michael Pedersen Kierkegaard, was a successful businessman, but that is pretty much where the feel-good part of his family story ends. By the time Søren was twenty-one years of age, his mother and five of his six siblings had passed away. His relationship with his surviving brother, Peter, remained rocky until his death. And, to further illustrate the personal difficulties of his early years, he became engaged to Regine Olsen* in 1840, only to break the engagement the following year. By the time Kierkegaard passed away at the age of forty-two, he had spent most of the inheritance left by his father and he had spent most of his social capital in a very public "attack" on the hypocrisy of Danish Christendom.*

Intellectually, however, Kierkegaard was a little more successful. He published his first book (*From the Papers of One Still Living*) three years before graduating from the University of Copenhagen with a theology degree. In 1843, two years after acquiring his degree, he launched what would become his recognized "authorship" with the publication of the two-volume *Either/Or*. Even though the sales of his books rarely reached five hundred copies during his lifetime, interest in his writings has continued to grow since the middle of the nineteenth century.

In the twentieth century, Kierkegaard was appropriated and interpreted for incredibly diverse purposes. At one end of the spectrum, some hailed his writings as the leading edge of a form of modern atheism known as existentialism.* At the other end, some praised him as the most important Christian critic of the secular rationalism of the Enlightenment.* The truth is somewhere between these extremes, but certainly closer to the latter than the former (as I hope to illuminate in this volume).[1] There is no hiding the fact that Kierkegaard was a critic of nineteenth-century Danish Christendom. Yet Kierkegaard intended his voice to be a corrective, to be used in the service of true Christianity. To begin to reveal this amid the often cryptic prose of Kierkegaard's *Fear and Trembling*, I would like to comment briefly on its idiosyncratic character and place in his authorship.

Fear and Trembling was published on October 16, 1843. It was a busy year for Kierkegaard—he had already launched his literary career with the publication of the massive two-volume *Either/Or* on February 20 and a short series of edifying discourses on May 16. On the same date that *Fear and Trembling* appeared, he also published *Repetition* and another short series of edifying discourses.[2] These were followed by yet another series of discourses on December 6. Further, in the subsequent year (1844), he published no less

1. I will gesture towards how some of the themes that have defined Kierkegaard historically are related to *Fear and Trembling* at the appropriate points in the text.

2. The short series of edifying or "upbuilding" discourses that appear with regularity in Kierkegaard's early authorship are published under his own name and are frequently developed around a biblical text. Further, they usually correspond thematically in one way or another to the respective pseudonymous writings. See Kierkegaard, *Eighteen Upbuilding Discourses*. According to Kierkegaard, they are published with the "gleam of the directly religious" that came to dominate his later writings. See Kierkegaard, *Point of View*, 7–8.

than six more volumes. Although his output slowed down a little in the following years, he continued to write with tremendous energy—either for publication or in his private journals and papers—until his death in 1855. Rarely has history seen an author as creative and prolific as Kierkegaard was in these years. Yet it was *Fear and Trembling* that Kierkegaard singled out as the text that would make him famous:

> Oh, once I am dead, *Fear and Trembling* alone will be enough for an imperishable name as an author. Then it will be read, translated into foreign languages as well. The reader will almost shrink from the frightful pathos in the book. But when it was written, when the person thought to be the author was going about in the incognito of an idler, appearing to be flippancy, wittiness, and irresponsibility personified, no one was able to grasp its earnestness. O you fools, the book was never as earnest as then. Precisely that was the authentic expression of the horror.[3]

One of the central themes of the book is faith and how much more difficult real faith is than assumed by Kierkegaard's contemporaries. In order to make his case, Kierkegaard appeals to the story of Abraham and Isaac contained in Genesis 22, the story in which Abraham—the hero of faith—is commanded to travel to Mt. Moriah in order to sacrifice his only son, Isaac. In this context, Kierkegaard argues that Abraham's willingness to kill his son cannot be "comprehended" or "understood" according to any reasonable or culturally acceptable Christianity. It is an ordeal that Abraham has to undertake alone with God. (But, as we shall see, sacrificing Isaac may not even be the most difficult part of the story to understand!)

3. Kierkegaard, *Journals and Papers*, VI 6491.

What Kierkegaard is targeting by framing Abraham in this manner is the domesticated Christianity of nineteenth-century Denmark, the state-sanctioned Christianity that had carefully arranged and articulated its theological commitments in a manner that did not demand anything of Christians beyond appropriate participation in Danish society. The story of Abraham, however, violates this sort of comfortable existence because it displays a God who demands that Abraham act as if he were a murderer. This demand is used by Kierkegaard to challenge his contemporaries to dare to live according to what they claim to believe, or at least to acknowledge their failure to live up to the demands of Christianity.

Another way of stating what Kierkegaard is trying to illuminate might be: he is more concerned with the *how* of Christianity than the *what* of Christianity—that is, he is more concerned about how Christianity ought to be lived than what propositional or speculative claims are made by Christians. Of course, he did not dispute the dogmatic content of the Lutheran Christianity in which he was raised. In fact, it is indispensable for his theology and ethics. But he believed that as long as Christianity was considered to be merely dogmatic content, it was not really Christianity. In his own words, he claimed, "My task has continually been to provide the existential-corrective."[4] He believed that as long as his contemporaries continued to speculate about the *what* of Christianity as if that was all that was required by God, they were deluding themselves. In his own way, Kierkegaard is appropriating the theme of "faith without works is dead"[5] that echoes through the Christian

4. Kierkegaard, *Journals and Papers*, I 708.

5. See Jas 2:14–26. In his late *For Self-Examination* Kierkegaard revisits the need to elevate the "minor premise" of Christianity, that is, the work of living Christianly. See *For Self-Examination*, 15–25.

tradition, from the early church to the twentieth-century examples of Dietrich Bonhoeffer* and Mother Teresa.*

Even if highlighting the dissonance between his contemporaries' lives and beliefs is one of Kierkegaard's central tasks in *Fear and Trembling*, there is still the matter of how to communicate this dissonance. Or, to rephrase in his terms, the further challenge of how to reintroduce faithful Christian existence into a Christendom in which everyone already thought they were Christians still remains. When *Fear and Trembling* was published, Kierkegaard was still relatively unknown as an author. In fact, he worked very hard to cultivate a public existence that did not reveal his identity as a passionate and prodigious writer in his early years. Hiding his identity in this way was part of the attempt to let his authorship speak on its own terms and convict its readers by surprise, "without authority."[6] Kierkegaard thought he could not simply begin by stating that his contemporaries were not Christians because that claim would fall on deaf ears—not only did his contemporaries believe that they were Christians, they were affirmed as such by the Danish Lutheran Church. In these early years of his authorship, therefore, he imaginatively sought to illuminate the disjunction between the lives of his contemporaries and faithful Christian existence from various perspectives. One could also say that he sought to remove his own identity

6. There is no doubt that Kierkegaard enjoyed the literary play in hiding his identity, and it is also quite likely that he used this as a ploy to generate interest in his works. As his authorship progressed, however, he articulated this authorial strategy as necessary to his role as an author. For example, in *The Point of View*, Kierkegaard comments that "without authority" is the category of his whole authorship. What he means by this is that he does not speak from a position of authority, that is, he is not a representative of the church and not an apostle. Therefore, he cannot make demands. Rather, he can only seek "to make one aware" of Christianity in other ways (e.g., prompt, induce, invite, etc.). See Kierkegaard, *Point of View*, 6, 118.

from *Fear and Trembling* so that his readers could identify with Abraham's ordeal without the undue distraction of Kierkegaard's personal life.[7] This appears to be at least one of the reasons that he published *Fear and Trembling* pseudonymously under the *nom de plume* Johannes *de silentio*, that is, John of silence or John the silent one.[8]

If one recognizes that Kierkegaard intended the book to be read as if written by another author, one can then begin to understand that it is important not to attribute any of the specific contents of *Fear and Trembling* directly to Kierkegaard without further explanation. Reflecting on his authorship later in life, he very clearly stated that "if it should occur to anyone to want to quote a particular passage from the [pseudonymous] books, it is my wish, my prayer, that he will do me the kindness of citing the respective pseudonymous author's name, not mine."[9] Of course, Johannes *de silentio* is Kierkegaard's invention and, therefore, everything found in the text is attributable to Kierkegaard in some fashion. But, what Kierkegaard means by insisting on the above qualification is that each pseudonym is created to write from a unique perspective and, therefore,

7. For better or worse, considerable energy has been spent attempting to read the text biographically, that is, attempting to read the text as a working out of Kierkegaard's broken engagement with Regine. See, for example, Hannay, *Kierkegaard: A Biography*, 191–93.

8. The use of pseudonyms was prevalent in Copenhagen's literary circles at the time. Kierkegaard embraced this tactic wholeheartedly, publishing both newspaper articles and books pseudonymously (partly to hide his own identity, partly to develop differing authorial points of view). Occasionally, he went as far as layering his pseudonymity. For example, Kierkegaard's *Either/Or* was allegedly published by Victor Eremita, but Eremita is little more than the editor of lengthy letters—perhaps "essays" would be more accurate—by "A," "B," and a couple of sermons by an unnamed "pastor in Jylland" that "B" sent to "A."

9. Kierkegaard, *Concluding Unscientific Postscript*, 627.

may not represent what Kierkegaard himself would say directly (remembering that Kierkegaard's intention here is to communicate indirectly). As we will discover, Johannes *de silentio* is a self-styled poet who is capable of describing Abraham's faith beautifully. But he is also completely incapable of following Abraham in the life of faith. This matters because it suggests that the author Kierkegaard may know more than the author Johannes *de silentio*, because the text is intentionally limited to a poetic perspective that is not particularly Christian. As I work through the text of *Fear and Trembling*, I will occasionally revisit the function of this unique perspective in the unfolding argument of the text.

Finally, please allow one further comment concerning the epigragh that sets the stage for the text that follows. The epigraph refers to an occasion of indirect communication between Tarquin the Proud (the last king of Rome) and his son through a messenger that merely recounted the actions of Tarquin to the son without understanding. No comment is provided to illuminate this cryptic tale even though it sets the tone for the entire text. I think one best grasps what Kierkegaard—and I am aware that I am attributing the epigraph to Kierkegaard and not to Johannes *de silentio*—is suggesting here if the epigraph is understood as a metaphor of the communicative task of *Fear and Trembling*. In the metaphor, Johannes *de silentio* is the unwitting messenger. The messenger cannot explain the actions of "Venerable Father Abraham" (19/22)—on that he remains silent. He can only recount the actions. Consequently, only the true children of Abraham, when informed of his actions by the messenger, will understand and obey the message despite the essential silence of the messenger concerning the meaning of the message.[10]

10. Another alternative is to attribute the epigraph to Johannes *de silentio* and/or Kierkegaard with Abraham playing the role of the

The epigraph is merely the first in a series of prefatory elements in *Fear and Trembling*. It is now time to take the plunge and let Johannes *de silentio* begin his own orientation to the particular problems and pathos of living faithfully and, therefore, to the particular problems and pathos that stand at the heart of Kierkegaard's authorship.

DISCUSSION QUESTIONS

1. Have you heard of Søren Kierkegaard before? If so, how was he described?

2. What, according to Kierkegaard, is the difference between the *what* and the *how* of Christianity? Is this a perennial concern, or is this a distinction tied to Kierkegaard's particular context?

3. What does it mean to speak about Christianity "without authority"? Why is this important to Kierkegaard? Why might this manner of speaking be important today too?

---

messenger. Understood this way, the epigraph would suggest an allegorical reading of the Abrahamic story as prefiguring Christianity (and especially the atonement or the sacrificial faith required of Christians). There is no doubt *Fear and Trembling* contains allusions to the New Testament, and it may be possible that these options need not be seen as mutually exclusive.

1

THE PREFACE

IF ONE ASSUMES THAT a Preface ought to state clearly the subject, plan, or purpose of a book, one will be sorely disappointed by the Preface offered at the beginning of *Fear and Trembling*. What one finds here instead is an oblique yet polemical commentary on the march of "modern philosophy." In its own way, however, the Preface does introduce key elements that constitute the subject and purpose of the larger text. In order to illuminate how this is the case, I would like to identify three themes in the Preface that run through the entire text (and large portions of Kierkegaard's corpus as well).

The first theme introduced is Johannes *de silentio*'s[1] condemnation of the relative ease with which one could acquire faith in nineteenth-century Denmark—faith is an idea that can be had "dirt cheap" (3/5). The economic language

1. From this point on, I will refer to Johannes *de silentio* (as *de silentio*) when I mean to indicate only the author of this particular text; I will refer to Kierkegaard when I mean to indicate the man behind the author and the author in the broader sense. Again, there is certainly overlap here. But since Kierkegaard intended to hide his identity from his readers (at least when *Fear and Trembling* was published), grasping the function of the text will sometimes require this sort of distinction even if it occasionally seems cumbersome.

and imagery used here to reinforce Kierkegaard's polemic also reappears at the beginning of the Epilogue, thereby bookending the entire argument of *Fear and Trembling*. Of course, concerns about cheap faith (usually parallel to concerns about cheap grace) have echoed throughout the Christian tradition since its very beginning.[2] The particular form of cheap faith that Kierkegaard was concerned about was that offered by his contemporaries whose theologies were deeply indebted to modern philosophy. To challenge his contemporaries, Kierkegaard uses *de silentio* to face them on their own terms, namely, within the framework of modern philosophy. But in order to gain some leverage, *de silentio* steps back to begin his argument with what he takes to be the foundation of modern philosophy, that is, the general assumption that modern philosophy begins with doubt.

That modern philosophy begins with doubt is, of course, a bit of a cliché that could be disputed. Nonetheless, *de silentio* appeals specifically to René Descartes* as the man who stands representatively at the beginning of modern philosophy, the first modern philosopher who is committed to beginning philosophy with doubt. The position in Descartes' thinking that *de silentio* has in mind is captured well in the following excerpt from *Meditations on First Philosophy*: "Anything which admits of the slightest doubt I will set aside just as if I had found it to be wholly false; and I will proceed in this way until I recognize something certain, or, if nothing else, until I at least recognize for certain that there is no certainty."[3] The Preface is not interested in praising doubt or modern philosophy in general; it is interested in praising Descartes for his humility and honesty in the face of this enormous task. Descartes, in

2. See, for example, Rom 6:1–3 and Jas 2:14–26.

3. Descartes, *Meditations on First Philosophy*, 16.

this way, serves as the benchmark against which *de silentio* critiques his contemporary lecturers, tutors, students, and dilettantes, who claim to have already gone beyond doubt in the service of extending the project Kierkegaard refers to as modern philosophy.

But how, exactly, is this critique related to cheap faith? In short, Kierkegaard perceived that some of his contemporaries understood Danish (or Germanic) cultural Christianity to be the actualization of reason in history. Therefore, his contemporaries could articulate how Christian faith necessarily belonged within a philosophy that allegedly began with doubt. This sort of faith would, of course, be cheap (by Kierkegaard's standards) because it would emerge in Danish thought and society simply as a matter of the unfolding of philosophical necessity in history. Faith would not be possessed individually in any meaningful way and it would not look anything like the faith required of Abraham.

The Preface then goes on to intimate that if one actually began one's philosophy with doubt, like Descartes, one would quickly discover that doubt cannot be overcome by anything other than divine revelation. Elsewhere in his writings, Kierkegaard emphatically argues that more knowledge does not conquer doubt; more knowledge simply provides more fuel for doubting.[4] If it accomplishes anything, doubt simply leads one to the recognition of one's ignorance. In this way, *de silentio* sets up the basic nondialectical* structure of the movement that undergirds *Fear and Trembling*. To state this movement specifically in terms of the Preface, the negative* movement of doubt does not necessarily or logically lead to the positive presence of faith;

4. Kierkegaard, *Journals and Papers*, I 776. For similar arguments written around this time, see also Kierkegaard, *Eighteen Upbuilding Discourses*, 125–39, and *Johannes Climacus*, which remained unpublished in his lifetime.

to restate generally with respect to the text as a whole, the negative movement of giving up something (e.g., Isaac) does not necessarily lead to receiving something back (e.g., Isaac). As we will see later in the text, this juxtaposition is captured most dramatically in the difference between the knight of resignation and the knight of faith.

A second theme introduced in the Preface is related to the first, and perhaps it is a deepening of the first—both doubt and faith are tasks "for a whole lifetime." According to *de silentio*, doubt was a lifelong task for "the ancient Greeks, who also surely understood a little about philosophy" (4/6). Faith was also a lifelong task for those tried and tested "old-sters" (especially Socrates) who lived in the "olden days" (5/7). What *de silentio* is driving at here is simply that doubt and faith are both ways of existing that require the continual disciplining of one's will in the desire for proficiency. Both require tremendous effort and entail tremendous costs. To be sure, doubt and faith are not the same ways of existing in terms of their material practices. But, formally, there are profound similarities in their rigorous requirements. Speaking particularly of faith, *de silentio* notes that proficiency is not a matter of understanding an idea but a matter of fighting the good fight in fear and trembling that "is not entirely outgrown by any person" (5/7). Again, this theme serves to indict his contemporaries, who arrogantly imagine themselves to not only have doubted everything but to have also moved beyond faith to the allegedly greater task of constructing a universal or comprehensive philosophy.[5]

Looking ahead specifically to the story of Genesis 22 and relating it to faith, it is clear that Abraham "is the father of all of us."[6] This is a theme that *de silentio* will

5. Representatives of this position whom Kierkegaard targets include Hegelians like Hans L. Martensen* and Johan Ludvig Heiberg.*

6. Rom 4:16.

return to repeatedly in the following pages. Yet, he is also adamant that sons and daughters do not inherit faith from their father. Yes, we may "see" more while standing on the shoulders of giants, but no giant can take one's place amid the everyday demands of life. Each child of each generation—and here Kierkegaard is speaking directly to his audience—must achieve a life of faith on his or her own. No more and no less is required.

To conclude, a third theme begins to take shape: *de silentio*, in choosing his particular style of writing, positions himself polemically against what he takes to be the problematic form of Danish philosophy—"the System." In one sense, the content of this theme seems to reiterate the criticisms that have served as the framework for orienting the entirety of the Preface. Yet, form and content are related for Kierkegaard, and it should come as no surprise that a critique of systematized or conceptual Christianity must take a form other than systematically addressing the alleged concepts of Christianity. Whether he maintains consistency on this point throughout is yet to be seen. But what we do see is a bit of the lyrical personality attributed to *de silentio*, who is not so silent in his critical appraisals. To bring the Preface to a conclusion, he offers no shortage of sarcasm in closing with the salutation "Respectfully" after not only disavowing "the System" but also mocking it and those who are invested in it.[7]

With these brief comments on the Preface, I have attempted to illuminate the polemical context in which Kierkegaard intended to place *Fear and Trembling*. In the process, I have also attempted to introduce the way in which Kierkegaard employs oppositional or dichotomous thinking in the service of delineating the differences between

---

7. These comments echo, in their own way, the concluding repartee in Hegel's Preface to *Elements of the Philosophy of Right*, 23.

what he understands to be the failures of Danish Christianity and true Christianity. And, finally, I believe the few scant pages of the Preface also provide a good indication of the manner in which Kierkegaard employs particular historical figures as (occasionally less than nuanced) representatives of philosophical or theological positions in order to illustrate that what is at stake in his argument are not mere ideas but the entirety of human existence. Of course, we have not yet been officially introduced to the central biblical figures that drive *Fear and Trembling*, so to those figures we will turn momentarily.

Before turning the page, perhaps one more very preliminary observation is in order: at no point does *de silentio*, the pseudonym, refer to faith as particularly Christian. We will find out much more about *de silentio* and what he means by "faith" in short order. For now, however, one general statement from Kierkegaard's later journals and papers will have to serve as a preliminary orientation: "Abraham is called the father of faith because he has the formal qualifications of faith, believing against the understanding, although it has never occurred to the Christian church that Abraham's faith had the content of the Christian faith."[8]

DISCUSSION QUESTIONS

1. Kierkegaard was concerned with a particular kind of "cheap faith" in his day. Is "cheap faith" something Christians ought to be worried about today?

2. In what way does *de silentio* hold up Descartes and Socrates as models for Christians to follow?

8. Kierkegaard, *Journals and Papers*, VI 6598.

3. Kierkegaard is often described in terms of existentialism, a form of philosophy that emphasizes the responsibility and will of an existing individual. Given what you
   have read thus far, why do you think he is frequently
   described this way?

2

TUNING UP

ALL THREE OF THE major "Abrahamic religions"—Judaism, Christianity, and Islam—trace their origins to Abraham in some way; Abraham has a significant part to play in the scriptures of each of these religions. The particular scriptural text that *de silentio* draws upon in this chapter recounts the most famous episode in Abraham's life. It is known as "the binding of Isaac" or the *Akedah* and it is found in Genesis 22:1–19. *De silentio* distills what he takes to be the narrative heart of the story in less than three lines:

> And God tested Abraham and said to him, take Isaac, your only son, whom you love, and go to the land of Moriah and offer him there as a burnt offering upon a mountain that I will show you. (8/10)

In assigning the title "Tuning Up" to this chapter, it is clear that *de silentio*'s purpose is to help his reader become attuned to Abraham. To do so, one might expect an explanation or description of Abraham that would increase the reader's understanding of his actions. That is not the case. In fact, *de silentio* chooses precisely the opposite strategy for attuning the reader to Abraham, that is, he works to illustrate that one cannot understand Abraham.[1] His strategy for rendering the story of Abraham in a manner that defies understanding is beautiful and exceptionally challenging at the same time.

First, the rhetoric or style of this chapter is unique, even for *Fear and Trembling*. It is structured as a fable—complete with a "once upon a time"—that begins with an anonymous child hearing the story of Abraham. The fable continues by explaining how this child continued to meditate on it throughout his life. Within this short story are nestled four pairs of reflections that represent ways in which the child, when grown, imagined the events on Mt. Moriah. Each pair of reflections consists of (*a*) one imaginative description of these events and (*b*) one parable or proverb concerning the weaning of a child. The short story that surrounds these reflections is simple enough to follow. But no further help in coming to grips with the relationship between the imaginative renderings of the binding of Isaac and the further comments concerning weaning a child is given by the author. And, by the end of the chapter, *de silentio*—whether intentionally or unintentionally—may leave one asking not only "who is able to understand [Abraham]?" (11/14) but also, who is able to understand this chapter?

Moving beyond the peculiar style of the chapter, the content here is poetically and intentionally opaque. I would like to suggest that perhaps the best question to ask concerning content is not what the various reflections reveal but what they do not reveal. Or, to restate, perhaps we should begin by asking, how do these reflections fail to tell the story of Abraham adequately? Asking this question will help us come to grips with what sort of "tuning up" *de*

1. And, of course, one can also find *de silentio*'s familiar mockery of those who claim to easily understand the story—in this case, those intellectuals who know Hebrew.

silentio is attempting to accomplish. Kierkegaard hints in this direction in his journals when he states that "Abraham was not great because he sacrificed Isaac but because he had faith, because he was cheerful and willing. That is what is accentuated in the four [reflections], for in each case he does it, but not in faith."[2]

In each of these imaginative reflections, there are three central characters: God, Abraham, and Isaac. Each of these characters has a relation with each of the others (for example, Abraham has a relationship with God and a relationship with Isaac). Against this backdrop, each of these reflections illustrates that Abraham, in the act of sacrificing Isaac, departs from his usual cheerful and willing faith in God (which is to say that each reflection reveals Abraham's lack of faith in a different way). As a matter of course, each of the reflections also illuminates how Abraham's lack of faith causes the relationships among the central characters to be destroyed.

That said, one caveat is in order before proceeding: any attempt to nail down an interpretation of these reflections to any one meaning is doomed to fail. At best, one can speculate what *de silentio* is driving at based on one's understanding of the larger context of the text. Therefore, please consider the following as merely a suggestive interpretation. After all, these reflections are created for the purpose of attuning, and part of that intended attuning is disorientation. With this in mind, I would like to provide a few observations on each reflection.

I. In this first reflection, Abraham chooses to become a "monster" in order to preserve Isaac's faith in God. Here, Isaac cannot "understand" Abraham's plan (and the term is repeated several times), so Abraham

2. Quoted in Kierkegaard, *Fear and Trembling* (Hong and Hong translation), 249.

chooses to claim that the sacrifice is actually his own desire and not God's command. In this way, Abraham destroys Isaac's trust and even appears to betray his own faith in God in an attempt to ensure that Isaac retains his faith in God. The language of a mother blackening her breast to wean her child in the ensuing parable reinforces this message, including the fact that the mother still looks at her child with a loving and tender gaze. At the end of the day, what we are presented with in this first reflection may not look like the worst outcome in pragmatic terms. In fact, it may even seem to suit our rather utilitarian world that cares more about outcomes than means, but it clearly is not the story contained in Genesis 22.

II. In this second reflection, *de silentio* appears to portray an Abraham who is silently obedient to God and yet ceases to love God. In this way, Abraham loses his father and Isaac does as well (and this is a very unfortunate way for a child to lose its mother). Again, the events are virtually the same. Yet, it is clear that obedience out of duty to a hidden and remote God is not necessarily the same thing as faith.

III. The third reflection is even less straightforward. There are several issues, including the juxtaposition of Abraham's treatment of Ishmael and Isaac. That said, one of the key issues here is that Abraham cannot reconcile loving his son with obedience to God. He, like nearly everyone else in the world, comes to the conclusion that killing one's son is a sin, a violation of one's duty to the son. Therefore, Abraham cannot reconcile what he takes to be a rather common ethical position with his love for God, who also demands his best. Amid these competing demands, Abraham sorrows with no peace of mind—eventually choosing his duty to his son. And it is precisely his desire to keep the child close that perpetuates his sorrow.

IV. Finally, in the fourth reflection, Abraham's despair is recognized by Isaac. Isaac loses his faith because the father had already lost his faith. In this case—in opposition to the first reflections—Isaac does not turn to God and essentially perishes.

In no way do these very preliminary comments capture the depth of *de silentio*'s poetic genius on display in this chapter. Nevertheless, my humble purpose here is twofold: (1) to suggest how we can begin to understand why Abraham would act as he does in each of these imagined scenarios, and (2) to highlight that *de silentio*'s exercise in "tuning up" is an exercise in challenging our preconceived notions about what constitutes Abraham's faith. Throughout, *de silentio* uses poetic means to gesture beyond the immediate actions associated with the trip to Mt. Moriah, where Abraham is prepared to sacrifice Isaac. He wants us to learn and to feel that Abraham's faith is *not* utilitarian, dutiful obedience, easily reconciled with the ethics of society, or driven by despair. Given the extensive energy devoted to preliminary orienting matters thus far in *Fear and Trembling*, however, one probably ought not to expect a quick resolution of the question that closes this chapter: "Who is able to understand [Abraham]?"

DISCUSSION QUESTIONS

1. In this section, *de silentio* creatively retells the story of Genesis 22 in many ways. Why does he do so?

2. Is it becoming clearer why Kierkegaard chose the pseudonym Johannes *de silentio* by this point? Explain.

3. How does this chapter differ from a sermon or academic commentary on Genesis 22?

3

A TRIBUTE TO ABRAHAM

In this last (or perhaps second-to-last) prefatory element of *Fear and Trembling*, *de silentio* finally begins to provide a positive account of Abraham's faith. Up to this point, he has been concerned with clearing the decks; now it is time to build again. To do so, he offers a "tribute" to Abraham. This tribute is an act of love, but it is also an act that sharply differentiates *de silentio* (a poet) from Abraham (a hero). In order to contextualize the relationship between the roles in which *de silentio* and Abraham are cast, I would like to step back and highlight the three sets of distinctions that undergird *de silentio*'s tribute.

First, despite the fact that *de silentio* claims there is more to existence than mere temporality in a rather roundabout way, it is important to notice that there is a sharp distinction between the eternal* and the temporal.* Kierkegaard is well aware of the fact that many of the ancient Greeks had an account of the eternal in one form or another.[1] For that reason, he systematically develops the

---

1. Here it almost appears that Abraham is cast within the categories of the ancient Greeks. The reason why this may be the case lies with Kierkegaard's use of the Greeks to argue with Hegel (and Danish Hegelians). Socrates is the central character for Kierkegaard

difference between what he takes to be the Socratic and the Christian ways of describing eternal consciousness a year later in *Philosophical Fragments*. At this point in *Fear and Trembling*, however, the fact that humans have an eternal consciousness is simply stated and linked to God's existence and actions.

Because humans have an eternal consciousness, human actions in temporality are not meaningless and hopeless. It almost seems that *de silentio* is indirectly suggesting something like God created heroes and poets to reveal the sorts of human actions that relate the eternal and the temporal meaningfully.[2] The hero and poet are united in this cause; they are united in their mutual dependence; they are united in their mutual service.

But, heroes and poets perform their service in different roles, hence the second distinction of the tribute—a hero acts, while a poet recollects. Through the poet's recollection it is possible for a hero to live in one time and yet speak to any time. After all, "thousands of years have elapsed" since the days of Abraham, and yet "every language commemorates" him to this day (19/23). The overarching purpose of *de silentio*'s tribute, then, becomes clearer: to praise Abraham rightly with his poetic gifts; the overarching purpose of Kierkegaard's design also becomes increasingly apparent:

---

in this debate and—in ways that parallel the appeals to the relationship between his contemporaries and Descartes and Abraham in *Fear and Trembling*—Kierkegaard later claims that "to go beyond Socrates when one nevertheless says essentially the same as he, only not nearly so well—that, at least, is not Socratic." See Kierkegaard, *Philosophical Fragments*, 111.

2. It may be helpful here to recall that *de silentio* does not necessarily speak for Kierkegaard, or rather he may say much less than Kierkegaard says in other places. *De silentio* is a kind of poet, and this sort of claim provides a profound legitimation for his posture in this text.

to provoke his contemporary reader into the possibility of a similar kind of relationship with God as God shared with Abraham.[3] We can see this explicitly near the end of the tribute when *de silentio* turns to address his reader directly: "You to whom my speech is addressed, was that the case with you? . . . When a call came to you, did you answer or not—perhaps softly and in a whisper? Not so Abraham" (18/21). No, Kierkegaard attributes to Abraham the response of "Here am I," the response claimed by other heroes of the faith in the Bible, including Jacob (Gen 31:11; 46:2), Moses (Exod 3:4), Samuel (1 Sam 3), and even Jesus (Heb 10:7, 9). Of course, we know the end of Abraham's story— "that it was only a test" (19/22)—but *de silentio*'s point is that you do not know the end of your story, and that is the only story you are called to live.

Throughout, however, it is important to remember that poetic recollection is not the same as heroic action. We will see shortly that *de silentio* confesses that he cannot imitate the faith of Abraham despite his tremendous praise for Abraham. In like manner, Kierkegaard indirectly invokes this same qualitative distinction against his contemporaries, who believe they have accomplished faith by merely describing it. In one of his late unpublished writings, Kierkegaard challenges the penchant for "wanting to reform [Christianity] without being willing to suffer and make sacrifices" by playing a rhetorical role very similar to that of *de silentio*. In "The Moral" of *Judge for Yourself!*, he states,

> If anyone among us dares to undertake to walk
> ethically in the character of what is suggested
> here, also appealing as a single individual to an
> immediate relationship with God, then I shall at

3. I say possibility here because that is all that the poet can do. Beyond creating the possibility, the poet cannot take any responsibility.

> once . . . be on duty to undertake what I under-
> stand before God as my task. My task will be:
> to escort him, the reformer, step by step, never
> leaving his side, in order to see if he step by
> step is in the character, is the extraordinary. If
> he should turn out to be that, then my escort-
> ing will be all bows and deference to him, the
> extraordinary—and, indeed, I venture to say of
> myself that among his contemporaries he will
> not find anyone, not a single one, who knows
> how to bow lower before the extraordinary.[4]

Kierkegaard continues, if for no other reason than it is clear to him that none of his contemporaries have the same faith as that of Abraham (and, in the later context, also Martin Luther): "But, but, if [the reformer] strays out of character, at that instant I will fall upon him."[5] These words by the late Kierkegaard are certainly more explicitly Christian than any *de silentio* would have written, but they still echo the sharp edge of Kierkegaard's critique of Danish Christendom contained within *de silentio*'s "Tribute to Abraham." The hero has to be willing to wait "a hundred years" before getting a son; the hero has to be willing to "draw the knife" before keeping Isaac (20/23). And, even then, one does not get further than faith.

The third and final set of distinctions that I would like to highlight are the distinctions in value ascribed to heroes. For *de silentio*, a hero is great according to what the hero loves, to what the hero expects, to what the hero struggles against, and to what the hero relies upon. The greatest hero of all will love God, expect the impossible, struggle with God, and rely entirely upon God. That is, at least in part, the story of Abraham according to *Fear and Trembling*. That

4. Kierkegaard, *Judge for Yourself!*, 211.
5. Ibid.

said, *de silentio* does not treat Abraham's life as if it is merely a single action; he goes on to examine the three pivotal and representative moments in Abraham's life in order to justify his conclusion—the call to travel to the promised land,[6] the promise of a son,[7] and the command to sacrifice Isaac.

In closing, I would like to return to comment once more on the distinction between the eternal and the temporal. In ways that will begin to make sense once one reads further into *Fear and Trembling*, the following claim is absolutely central to grasping the text: "It is great to lay hold of the eternal, but it is greater to stick doggedly to the temporal after having given it up" (15/18). What *de silentio* is attempting to articulate here in brief is that Abraham's faith is "for this life" (17/20). It is a faith that gives up the temporal and chooses the eternal—that is, chooses faith in God—while also believing that, somehow, God will honor the temporal, God will provide in the temporal. It is a faith that is not only for a future life, for that is not really faith.

De silentio's faith is not, however, another version of the "health and wealth" gospel. As noted above, there is no logical way to map the relationship between the temporal and the eternal ahead of time, no economic equation to ensure a return balance in temporality. And, unsurprisingly, the next chapter immediately opens by returning again to this theme.

DISCUSSION QUESTIONS

1. Why does *de silentio* describe Abraham as a "hero" of faith? How is this different from a "poet" of faith? How are both of these relevant to contemporary Christians?

---

6. See Gen 12:1–8.
7. See Gen 17:1–8; 18:1–15; and 21:1–7.

2. To what end is *de silentio* utilizing the distinction between the temporal and the eternal? Is this how Christians talk today?

3. What does *de silentio* mean when he talks about faith "for this life?"

4

A PRELIMINARY OUTPOURING FROM THE HEART

READING KIERKEGAARD SOMETIMES FEELS like swimming in a whirlpool—one keeps going round and round in circles and all one can think of is not drowning. If read slowly, however, it becomes clear that it is precisely in this chapter that *de silentio*'s line of argument (to use the phrase loosely) begins to coalesce and crystallize. What I mean by this statement is that it is in this chapter that the various poetic explorations, polemical overstatements, and peculiar distinctions that *de silentio* has energetically explored in the preliminary parts of *Fear and Trembling* are finally organized and aligned according to one basic distinction, namely, the difference between infinite resignation and faith.

Before jumping too far ahead too quickly, however, please allow me to begin with a few comments on the role that this chapter plays within *Fear and Trembling*. This will set the background against which I outline the manner in which *de silentio* sketches the newly refined contrast between infinite resignation and faith. Once this step is complete, I will then be able to provide a critical summary of the claims contained in *de silentio*'s argument thus far. In this way, a relatively firm platform emerges from which one can begin to relate *de silentio*'s portrayal of faith to his Lutheran context.

After *de silentio*'s "Tribute to Abraham," we finally arrive at what could be considered the heart of *Fear and Trembling*, that is, the section devoted to three pivotal "Problems." That said, this chapter—"A Preliminary Outpouring from the Heart"—is not yet one of these problems. Rather, the reader finds herself again wrapped up in another introductory chapter, although this time *de silentio* provides some rationale for why he has spent so much time developing the oppositional distinctions thus far. In short, each of the problems to be examined in the following chapters emerges because of the specific quality of the relationship between the aforementioned distinctions: "It is now my intention to draw out in the form of problems the dialectical factors implicit in the story of Abraham in order to see what a prodigious paradox* faith is" (46/53).

A paradox is generally defined as a statement that seems to be self-contradictory. We have seen *de silentio* working in this direction for some time. But he is not interested in a generic understanding of faith as paradoxical (which is to say that he is not interested in merely claiming that faith is absurd*); *de silentio* is interested in the very particular dialectical factors that constitute the paradox of faith (which is to say that he is interested in claiming that faith contains a very particular kind of absurdity). And, therefore, it seems fairly clear that the purpose of this chapter is to explain what exactly is paradoxical about Abraham's faith.[1]

1. For much of the twentieth century, Kierkegaard was identified

⌒

To begin the chapter, *de silentio* returns to the qualitative difference between the visible and the spiritual worlds. These worlds operate according to different laws: in the first, toil is rewarded randomly (as we see every day); in the second, toil is perfectly and divinely rewarded (in ways we cannot see). Even though *de silentio* here returns to the economic imagery he began with, this is a truncated return. *De silentio*'s intention is not to explain what sort of rewards spiritual toil receives but merely to assert that there is no spiritual reward if there is no spiritual toil. And there is no spiritual toil without anxiety, without sleepless nights, without reading the story of Abraham as an ordinary story—a story that takes time, a story with real people, real relationships, and real expectations, a story that includes a demand that a father literally sacrifice his son.

In short, *de silentio* is driving the point that it requires spiritual toil to arrive at the conclusion that there are only two contradictory ways to describe Abraham's action: either it is murder (the ethical expression) or it is a sacrifice (the religious expression). And Abraham's situation is difficult

---

with an existential "leap of faith," irrationalism, and the celebration of the absurd. The range of agreement on this matter was tremendously diverse, from Francis Schaeffer, on one hand, to Jean-Paul Sartre, on the other. Albert Camus, in *The Myth of Sisyphus*, presents perhaps the most articulate argument to this effect. Camus states, "For [Kierkegaard], too, antinomy and paradox become criteria of the religious. . . . Christianity is the scandal, and what Kierkegaard calls for quite plainly is the third sacrifice required by Ignatius Loyola, the one in which God most rejoices: 'The sacrifice of the intellect.'" See Camus, *Myth of Sisyphus*, 36.

I hope it is clear, by the end of this volume, that Kierkegaard is not interested in sacrificing the intellect in any general way. In this and subsequent chapters, I intend to show that his employment of "paradox" and "the absurd" is very specific and aimed towards a particular kind of immanent dialectical logic.

because there is no visible evidence to justify why his plan is not murder. This, for *de silentio*, is how to begin talking about faith in the right way. One can well imagine that he pauses so long to depict this step because his comments function as yet another criticism of the this-worldly nature of nineteenth-century Danish Christendom, the age that is "too tenacious of life to die" (35/42).[2]

Once one has worked through the pathos required to grasp that Abraham is considered a murderer according to the ethics of Danish (and pretty much any ordered) society—even while he is still a man of faith—a further step is possible. *De silentio* then subtly introduces a second yet profoundly important distinction—the distinction between sacrificing Isaac and receiving Isaac back. This is the "double movement" (29/36) that Abraham makes, and it provides the paradigmatic framework for understanding the movements of the "knight of resignation" and the "knight of faith." With the introduction of this double movement, *de silentio* sharpens his definition of what constitutes Abraham's faith—it is no longer merely his willingness to sacrifice Isaac (the first movement of infinite resignation) but also and necessarily his belief that he will receive Isaac back (the second movement of faith). According to *de silentio*, this second movement of belief and trust makes no sense because there is no earthly calculus that could yield such a result. This belief is, in his words, absurd. This is what he refers to as the "dialectic of faith" (30/36).[3]

---

2. This is also to say that *de silentio* believes his contemporary world would unquestioningly consider Abraham a murderer if they actually encountered him. Because of this, they are merely "wallflowers" at the dance of infinity (34/41).

3. It is important to note that *de silentio* believes this type of dialectic to be precisely the opposite of Hegel's dialectic (and Greek dialectic). *De silentio* goes to great lengths to describe the contrast: in the dialectic of faith there is no intrinsic or logical relationship

At first glance, one may wonder why *de silentio* is so interested in claiming that Abraham's willingness to sacrifice Isaac in itself is not an act of faith, for this is often how the story is recounted. The answer is complicated. What Kierkegaard saw and sought to communicate through *de silentio* was something that our society sometimes loses sight of, that is, not all sacrifices are equal. *De silentio* has already provided a hint in this direction with his claim that the hero who struggles with God is greater than the hero who struggles with the world or with himself. As we will see, the hero who struggles with the world is a tragic hero.[4] Shortly, *de silentio* will bring forward Agamemnon* as a classic example of the tragic hero. According to Greek mythology, Agamemnon sacrificed his daughter, Iphigenia, to Artemis in order to appease the goddess so that she would allow his fleet to continue their journey to the battle of Troy. This sort of hero can be understood by the poet *de silentio* because Agmemnon's sacrifice was performed solely for the purpose of a particular earthly goal. But, as we shall see, Agamemnon is not Abraham. Abraham's sacrifice entails no visible or temporal purpose.

Another issue that drives the distinction between infinite resignation and faith lurks in the background of *Fear and Trembling*—the person of Socrates. Two years before *Fear and Trembling* was published, Kierkegaard defended his dissertation titled *The Concept of Irony*. In it, Socrates is cast as the first person to separate himself as an individual from his society, the first person to employ the negative— the first movement of faith (in the form of irony*)—against

---

between the movements; in the Hegelian dialectic, the second movement is necessarily determined by the first movement (that is, the second movement is immanent negatively in the first).

4. See the introduction of this term in Kierkegaard, *Fear and Trembling*, 28/34.

his contemporary world.[5] In the process, Kierkegaard notes that Socrates also gained eternal consciousness. But, Socrates was not a man of faith (at least not in the sense that *de silentio* is talking about).[6] It is against this backdrop that one can begin to make sense of why *de silentio* describes resignation (which is a kind of negation of the finite world) as separate from faith. The following statement from the chapter sharply illustrates the difficulty Socrates poses for *de silentio*: "The act of resigning does not require faith, for what I gain in resignation is my eternal consciousness, and that is a purely philosophical movement which I take comfort in making when required and which I can discipline myself to do" (41/48).

One more observation should also be noted before moving on. As even a casual reader will notice at this point, the notion of sacrifice has become a bit indefinite. After all, Abraham does not actually kill Isaac on Mt. Moriah. Therefore, the physical action of sacrificing can no longer be definitive; the spiritual movement of resignation has taken its place as the first movement toward faith. Resignation, therefore, occurs in the world of spiritual toil.[7]

5. Socrates plays this role for Hegel as well (and Kierkegaard is borrowing from Hegel here while also attempting to internally challenge him). See Hegel, *Elements of the Philosophy of Right*, 166–67.

6. This is not to say, however, that Socrates does not express some form of religiousness. In the pseudonymous *Philosophical Fragments* and *Concluding Unscientific Postscript*, Kierkegaard describes the immanent religiousness of Socrates under the category of Religiousness A (which is qualitatively different from the paradoxical religion of Religiousness B, a form of Christianity). See Kierkegaard, *Concluding Unscientific Postscript*, 561–86.

7. This is an articulation of the same conviction that leaves Kierkegaard ambivalent about monasticism, which is expressed well in his journals: "Meanwhile I willingly concede the dubiousness of the monastic movement, for it went too far in externalizing what ought to be inward." See Kierkegaard, *Journals and Papers*, III 2749.

The imaginary story *de silentio* relates about the knight of resignation and his princess makes this very clear as well. One may also think of the "peace and rest" (38/45) found in Stoicism* as another example of what *de silentio* has in mind here. In the knight of resignation we see—as we saw in Socrates and Descartes—that proper negation requires discipline for a lifetime (whether the negation finds its expression in doubt, irony, or resignation). Further, we find that this resignation is qualified as infinite in two ways: (*a*) it resigns the value of the finite (temporal) and accepts the value of the infinite (the eternal); and (*b*) there is no "to a certain extent" in the resignation, which is to say that the resignation is infinite, total.

Therefore, Abraham's happy reception of Isaac back into the temporal world of familial relations is necessarily jarring to the knight of resignation because it requires an entirely different kind of movement than resignation. The second movement of faith is a movement of reception, openness, humility, and lack of control. This is, therefore, a "higher" movement, as it is "miraculous." *De silentio* describes well what he takes to be the difficulty in the following statement:

> The knight of faith is the only happy person and heir to the finite, while the knight of resignation is a stranger and a foreigner. To get the princess in this way, to live joyfully and happily day in and day out with her (for it is also conceivable that the knight of resignation could get the princess but his soul had clearly perceived the impossibility of their future happiness), so as to live joyfully and happily every moment by virtue of the absurd, every moment to see the sword hanging over the beloved's head and yet to find,

not rest in the pain of resignation, but joy by virtue of the absurd—that is miraculous. (43/50)[8]

This is, according *de silentio*, the particular paradox of faith.

～

In this chapter, *de silentio* has claimed to depict Abraham's
faith in the manner that it demands: either we must forget
Abraham or we must learn to be horrified by the paradox
that is the meaning of his life. In this way, *de silentio* has
sought to counter the "cheap edition of Abraham" that Kierkegaard thought was being peddled in Copenhagen at the
time.

In the above comments, I have attempted to present
de silentio's project within at least a few aspects of its intellectual context. What I have not yet pointed out, however,
is that Kierkegaard is also placing *de silentio*'s task within a
rather familiar biblical frame. Although *de silentio* is allegedly not a man of faith, he certainly is familiar with biblical
imagery and allusion. Gestures to themes in the Old and
New Testaments permeate the text. Yet, one very important
text that echoes throughout *Fear and Trembling* remains
unstated. That text is Matthew 16:24–25 and it attributes
the following to Jesus: "If any want to become my followers,
let them deny themselves and take up their cross and follow

8. *De silentio* confesses that he has never found a person like this,
but he imaginatively describes the man of faith as one who "looks
just like a tax collector," one who "belongs entirely to the world; no
bourgeois philistine could belong to it more" (32/39). Whatever one
makes of this description (and it has generated considerable debate),
it coheres with the double movement of faith described in *Fear and
Trembling*. Later, Kierkegaard slowly moves toward identifying Christian faith with suffering, though even that suffering may be hidden in
its own way as well. As we will see in the forthcoming companion
volume (devoted to *Works of Love*), this is one of the many themes
that will reappear in *Works of Love*.

me. For those who want to save their life will lose it, and those who lose their life for my sake will find it."

To deny oneself first, to doubt the world's wisdom first, to resign the things that the world values first—only then will one truly receive one's life in faith. This is the heart of the polemical message *de silentio* attempts to communicate in this chapter. Several years later, Kierkegaard recounted a similar message in his journal:

> The matter is quite simple. In order to have faith, there must first be existence, an existential qualification.
>
> This is what I am never sufficiently able to emphasize—that to have faith, before there can even be any question about having faith, there must be the *situation*. And this situation must be brought about by an existential step on the part of the individual.
>
> We have completely done away with the propaedeutic* element. We let the individual go on in his customary mediocre rut—and so he gets faith by and by, just about the way one can learn lessons word-perfect without needing the situation.[9]

Or, in short, faith is for this world. But it can only be faith once one is no longer beholden to this world. One must give up one's life in order to find faith. In this way, we see once again that Kierkegaard is more interested in the *how* of Christianity than the *what*. Faith is not merely a form of knowledge or belief, though it is a way of existing that assumes belief; faith does not merely precede works, though works flow from faith; above all, faith is a way of existing that passes understanding not through what it

---

9. Kierkegaard, *Journals and Papers*, II 1142.

knows but by how it trusts, how it humbles itself, and how it receives "every good and perfect gift from the Father of lights."[10]

On the surface, this is not the caricature of Luther's *sola fide*, of justification "by faith alone." Kierkegaard is well aware that his form of Lutheranism is not exactly the same as that of his contemporaries.[11] But Kierkegaard is also not willing to hand over the authority of Luther too quickly. In *For Self-Examination*, he appeals to the example of Luther in support of a restless faith, the Luther whose "life expressed works,"[12] the Luther who spent years in a cloister cell "in fear and trembling and much spiritual trial"[13] before daring to proclaim that a person is saved by faith alone. That is, according to Kierkegaard, the real Luther: Luther's life was consumed by fearfully working out his salvation in preparation for the proclamation of justification by faith alone.

Again, there is much more to Kierkegaard than *de silentio*. For example, one could turn to another discourse published by Kierkegaard the same day as *Fear and Trembling* entitled "Strengthening in the Inner Being" to find a fuller account of God's role in the reception of faith; one

---

10. See Jas 1:17–21, the text that Kierkegaard refers to as his favorite passage of scripture. Through the years, he returned to write multiple upbuilding discourses on this text. See Bauckham, *James*, 158–73.

11. See, for example, his caustic comment recorded in his journals: "What a relief for the person who hears and reads the contemporary pastors and almost has to say to himself, 'I understand from you what I am to do—simply take it easy, because I have already become too perfect'—what a relief to read Luther. There is a man who can really stay by a person and preach him farther out instead of backwards." See Kierkegaard, *Journals and Papers*, III 2466.

12. Kierkegaard, *For Self-Examination*, 16.

13. Ibid., 19.

could also look to *Philosophical Fragments* to find a fuller argument to the same effect. In the second volume we will also find that faith is important to the argument of *Works of Love*. But to attempt to move beyond *de silentio*'s description too quickly is to undermine the foundation of the particular political arguments he will make in the remaining chapters.

DISCUSSION QUESTIONS

1. What does *de silentio* mean when he describes faith as a "prodigious paradox?" Why is this definition so important?

2. What is the difference between the knight of resignation and the knight of faith? And why does one have to be the former before becoming the latter?

3. *De silentio* also makes a comparison between Abraham and the tragic hero. How is this distinction relevant to how Christians think about their place in politics or society more broadly considered?

5

PROBLEM I

HERE WE BEGIN THE heart of *Fear and Trembling*. Finally *de silentio* introduces the first of three problems that will occupy the bulk of the remainder of the text. Having struggled through the many-layered introduction, one should feel prepared (or at least rightly oriented) to face these problems head-on. Of course, this section of text—which I will henceforth refer to as a chapter because it is a sufficiently discrete argument to be treated as such—is no easier to grapple with than any of the previous.

There are essentially (though unofficially) two parts to the chapter that address Problem I.[1] First, *de silentio* answers the posed question theoretically; second, *de silentio* answers the question through biographical illustrations. In the first part, we find something like an organized argument against a Hegelian point of view; in the second part, we find comparisons between Abraham and other characters of historical renown that illuminate Abraham's

---

1. *De silentio* does not divide the chapter formally. In order to understand the logic of Problem I, however, I suggest that one think of the beginning of page 50 in the Evans and Walsh edition (the middle of page 57 in the Hong and Hong translation) as the point at which *de silentio* revisits the argument of the previous pages in a new vein.

paradoxical faith. To that end, *de silentio* highlights differences with Agamemnon, Jephthah,* and Brutus,* and similarities with the Virgin Mary and Christ. Despite the shape of the question that begins the chapter, the basic tension that drives the chapter is the contest between the primacy of an individual's relationship to God (the one) and an individual's relationship to one's community (the many). The terminology employed by *de silentio* is the language of the particular and the universal because this argument amounts to an attempt to use Hegelian language against the Hegelian point of view. There are several other Hegelian terms that are introduced to reinforce his critique and these will be taken up as the argument progresses. I would like to tackle each of the chapter's two parts separately for the purpose of tracing the central argument from start to finish. Problem I is compact so I will take the time necessary to unpack its argument in some detail.

∾

The question that defines this section seems straightforward enough: "Is there a teleological suspension of the ethical?" (46/54). The short answer to the problem is yes, in the case of Abraham there is a teleological suspension of the ethical (49/56). But deciphering what, exactly, this statement means is a little less straightforward. To help make sense of *de silentio*'s claim, I will highlight the major premises that undergird the logic of the argument contained in the first section of this chapter. In this way, I expect that you will find some clarity concerning the terms of the argument and its conclusion.

A word of warning up front: the position outlined at the beginning of Problem I is not Kierkegaard's point of view; this position is an abbreviated and approximated form of Hegel's point of view that *de silentio* will then oppose with the example of Abraham.[2]

Premise 1: The ethical is the universal. The first statement offered by *de silentio* after posing the question is that "the ethical as such is the universal" (46/54). What *de silentio* means by "the ethical" is not what is commonly understood today when we use the term "ethical." In this context, *de silentio* is referring to what German philosophy termed *Sittlichkeit** or social ethics. Specifically, this is a term that refers to the ethical responsibilities one has as one plays one's everyday role in society, and perhaps the Protestant notion of vocation vaguely resembles this concept. This form of ethics is different from (and sometimes in opposition to) personal or individual morality, for which the term *Moralität** was used. Therefore, what we have in this statement is not something that *de silentio* (or Kierkegaard) is making up on his own but simply a foundational statement that begins to answer the problem by starting with the presupposition entailed within one of the key philosophical terms in the question, namely, "the ethical."

But why then would the ethical be described as universal? Again, the answer lies in *de silentio's* representation of a Hegelian point of view (and we are alerted to the fact that he is thinking primarily of Hegel's *Elements of the Philosophy of Right* on the very next page). According to a Hegelian point of view, the ethical is universal in the sense that it applies to everyone at all times, which is another way of saying that one expresses one's individual duties and

2. Another word of warning: Hegel is, of course, much more complicated than what is represented here, so please do not assume sufficient familiarity with Hegel on the basis of reading *Fear and Trembling*. What *de silentio* is driving at is a very basic difference between Abraham (as portrayed in *Fear and Trembling*) and Hegel that is frequently, though not universally, understood to be an actual difference.

rights concretely in society according to that society's laws and customs without exception. For Hegel, the ethical is the highest sphere where subjective and abstract individual wills[3] are given concrete expression in a manner that coincides with the communal will of a society.[4] For example, in *Elements of the Philosophy of Right* he states, "Hence *duty* and *right* coincide in this identity of the universal and the particular will, and in the ethical realm, a human being has rights in so far as he has duties, and duties in so far as he has rights."[5] Or, as *de silentio* would like to highlight, according to this understanding of the ethical, an individual has no rights that contradict the individual's duties to society (which is simply a fancy way of saying that a reasonable individual would necessarily find his or her will in accord with the universal will of the society).

Premise 2: There is no telos outside the ethical. This premise is related to the first one and, in short, *de silentio* means that a Hegelian version of the ethical—as the sphere of concrete social ethics—is the final end or goal of human existence. That is, there is no higher purpose for an individual than to "express himself" in the ethical, to "annul his particularity in order to become the universal" (46/54). Or, to use Hegel's words to express what *de silentio* is attempting to capture, an individual's self-consciousness only finds its substantial freedom when it has "the state as its essence, its end, and the product of its activity."[6]

---

3. Think, for example, of "the will to do good." No matter how deeply I desire to do good, this desire is simply an abstract expression of my individual will.

4. This is the step where "the will to do good" is expressed concretely in social relations. In our society, obeying a summons for jury duty would be one example. Caring for, feeding, and educating one's son or daughter would be another excellent example.

5. Hegel, *Elements of the Philosophy of Right*, 197.

6. Ibid., 275.

Premise 3: To assert one's particularity against the universal is sin. At first blush, this statement may appear entirely reasonable. If the ultimate purpose of human existence is participation in the universal demand of the ethical, then resisting this purpose must be described negatively in one way or another. Hegel recognized this and defined the act of giving precedence to one's particularity over against the universal as one's capability for being evil.[7] In essence, evil is equated with breaking or not fulfilling the laws and customs of one's society. In his *Elements of the Philosophy of Right*, Hegel also notes that Socrates and the Stoics are examples of moral individuals who tended to look inwards into the self for what is right and good.[8] But, he then continues, "Once self-consciousness has grasped and acquired its formal right in this way, everything depends on the kind of content which it gives to itself."[9] Or, to restate, if one does not express one's self-consciousness with the right kind of content—that is, in the ethical—then one sins.

We will revisit these premises frequently throughout the remainder of *Fear and Trembling* because *de silentio* takes these to be the foundational commitments of the point of view he opposes. But before moving too quickly, please allow me to pause for a moment to note the corollary that *de silentio* develops out of these premises in this particular chapter.

Corollary: Participation in the ethical has the same character as gaining eternal salvation. To arrive at this

---

7. Ibid., 167.

8. This is one of the central reasons why rightly describing the activities of these characters is so important to Kierkegaard as well.

9. Ibid., 166. The language here may help explain why *de silentio* has used phrases like "eternal consciousness" in a manner that seems somewhat arbitrary if one is unaware of the Hegelian and Greek backdrop to *Fear and Trembling*.

conclusion, *de silentio* employs a little syllogistic reasoning. What he means by this claim is simply that statement (A) *the ethical is the telos of human existence* formally parallels statement (B) *eternal salvation is the telos of human existence*. Statement (A) is Hegel's claim, while statement (B) is a generic claim that was generally held in some form by most Christians in Danish Christendom (although this statement is simply implied by *de silentio* as common knowledge). To hold both claims as valid, however, would yield (C) *eternal salvation is the same as (or is found in) the ethical*. It is precisely this corollary that alarms Kierkegaard because this is not merely a statement that encourages one to obey the law; this is a statement that equates a particular social existence with salvation, with a completely realized eschatology. And if the latter is the case, then salvation is found in nothing but the willful embrace of the laws and customs of one's society.

On the Contrary: But Hegel is wrong! This *sed contra* statement captures the central evaluative point of Problem I. Why exactly is Hegel wrong? Simply put, Hegel's articulation of the ethical (at least as summarized by *de silentio*) cannot account for the paradoxical faith of Abraham that was examined in detail in the previous chapter.[10] And if

10. *De silentio* states his indictment of Hegel by arguing that Hegel should have protested Abraham's esteemed role as the father of faith. He frames his criticism in this way because Hegel is relatively silent about Abraham. In comparison, Immanuel Kant* (an immediate precursor that both Hegel and Kierkegaard read extensively) was boldly willing to suggest that Abraham was not only unreasonable but also misguided: "For as regards the theistic miracles, reason can at least have a negative criterion at its disposal, namely, if something is represented as commanded by God in a direct manifestation of him yet is directly in conflict with morality, it cannot be a divine miracle despite every appearance of being one (e.g. if a father were ordered to kill his son who, so far as he knows, is totally innocent)." See Kant, *Religion within the Boundaries of Mere Reason*, 100.

Abraham is the model of faith for Christians—he is "Venerable Father Abraham," after all—then Hegel's articulation of the ethical cannot account for Christianity any more than it can account for Abraham.

De silentio is careful to remind his reader that Abraham was not Socrates nor a Stoic who refused to make the movement from particularity into the ethical. Abraham already lived according to and embraced the universal requirements of the ethical—after all, he worked for a living, he loved his wife, and he loved his son—until he was called to sacrifice Isaac.[11] His willingness to sacrifice Isaac is a willingness to suspend the ethical and its requirements for a higher *telos*, namely, obedience to God. To place obedience to the ethical before or above this would be tantamount to idolatry. Therefore, to reiterate the answer to the question stated at the beginning of the chapter: the story of Abraham contains a teleological suspension of the ethical. This is a result of the paradoxical nature of Abraham's faith. Claiming that Hegel is wrong, however, is still different than claiming to understand Abraham. This distinction is important for *de silentio* because he seeks to preserve Abraham from the universality of the ethical.

Therefore Abraham's faith cannot be mediated. As we have seen in the introductory sections of *Fear and Trembling*, there is no universal or ethical logic that can explain Abraham's action. That is, his willingness to sacrifice is not undertaken for an earthly *telos*; his willingness to sacrifice Isaac is not, as Hegel would have it, an expression of the obedience that is the condition "upon which the [Jewish] nation continues in the state in which it is."[12] There is no

11. Recall the importance of noting that the life of faith is a cheerful existence previously discussed in chapter 2.

12. See Hegel, *Lectures on the Philosophy of Religion*, 2:216. Much more could and should be said about the relevance of Hegel's *Lectures*

category that one can insert (the good of the community, the good of the state, or even the good of the church, for example) as a middle term to link his actions back to the ethical. Problem III will return to this theme with a vengeance. In this chapter, however, *de silentio* merely concludes that admiration of Abraham is demented in a certain sense.

~

After having clearly stated his argument concerning Abraham's teleological suspension of the ethical in the first part of this chapter, *de silentio* then broadens the horizon of the question in the subsequent pages. In an attempt to provide a loose structure for coming to grips with the remaining pages of Problem I, I will comment briefly on the relationship between Abraham and the other characters *de silentio* introduces for comparison.

The first contrasting character to appear is Agamemnon. As indicated earlier, Agamemnon sacrificed his daughter Iphigenia to appease an angry Artemis. But it is not merely to appease Artemis; it is ultimately for an ethical *telos*, namely, fair winds for sailing to the battle of Troy. This sacrifice is tragic, no doubt, as *de silentio* illustrates poetically.[13] Yet, Agamemnon sacrifices his daughter magnanimously and heroically on behalf of the ambitions of Greece. According to Hegel's development of the ethical, the good of the state (in this case, Greece) is a higher form of the

---

on the Philosophy of Religion to the material contained in *Fear and Trembling*. Given the limits of this volume, however, I have chosen to focus my commentary on Kierkegaard and Hegel primarily through *Elements of the Philosophy of Right* because it is the text that appears explicitly in *Fear and Trembling*.

13. It is important to note that Kierkegaard has in mind the version of this tragedy provided in Euripides' *Iphigenia at Aulis* (76/87).

ethical than the good of the family (in this case, Iphigenia).[14] *De silentio* understands this well and therefore concludes that while Agamemnon violates his ethical responsibilities to his daughter, this suspension of the ethical is taken up again in a higher expression of the ethical: "The tragic hero still remains within the ethical" (51/59). Therefore, there is no teleological suspension of the ethical in Agamemnon's sacrifice. Agamemnon is no Abraham.

The Old Testament also provides an illustration somewhat analogous to Agamemnon in the person of Jephthah the judge. In short, Jephthah was about to lead Israel into battle with the Ammonites when he made an oath that he would sacrifice "whoever comes out of the doors of my house to meet me" when he returned victorious.[15] The arrangement is simple: victory from God in exchange for a sacrifice from his own household. Upon returning triumphantly, Jephthah is met by his daughter, his only child. Like Iphigenia, Jephthah's daughter embraces her service to the nation because she understands that her death serves the greater communal good, a higher expression of the ethical. But what if Jephthah had simply come home one day and, for no apparent reason, said to his daughter, "Grieve for two months and then I will sacrifice you" (51/58)? This apparently unjustified action would change the story completely; this version would make the story as difficult to understand as the story of Abraham; this version would open the door for a teleological suspension of the ethical into the story. But Jephthah is no Abraham.

Finally, and to belabor the point, *de silentio* introduces the actions of Lucius Junius Brutus, a onetime consul of Rome. Brutus's sons were involved in a political conspiracy

14. See the development of these stages in Part 3 of Hegel's *Elements of the Philosophy of Right*.

15. See Judg 11:29–40.

and, as a result, Brutus was required to put them to death. Of these three comparisons, this is probably the most understandable for us today because we generally appreciate the rule of law. And it most aptly expresses the triumph of the universality of the laws of the nation over particularity. But Brutus is no Abraham.

In contrast to these three tragic heroes, Abraham's greatness lies in his particular personal virtue. A category other than "the ethical" is needed to praise Abraham's faith. *De silentio* then formulates an expression for Abraham's posture that has become identified with Kierkegaard ever since: "The single individual places himself in an absolute relation to the absolute" (54/62). In this relation there are no visible justifications and no assured outcomes. It is—as Kierkegaard is fond of saying—like swimming out where the water is 70,000 fathoms.

Despite the fact that *de silentio*'s polemical resistance to his age dominates quite a few pages at this point, it would be a mistake to conclude that the role of this chapter is solely to critique, to challenge, to negate. The closing gestures in a positive direction do not constitute direct explanations by *de silentio*. The poetic gestures toward the actions of Mary and Christ do seem to imply more than *de silentio*, the non-Christian pseudonym, is capable of saying.

Certainly, the story of the angel Gabriel visiting Mary to tell her that she would be the mother of Jesus is quite different from the story of Abraham.[16] Yet they are similar formally in several ways that *de silentio* believes to be important. First, they begin in private with a divine communication that cannot be explained. Mary too places herself in an absolute relation to the absolute. Both stories contain distress, anxiety, and paradox; both Mary and Abraham became greater through distress, torment, and paradox. And,

16. See Luke 1:26–38.

in a manner that is absolutely essential to the argument of *Fear and Trembling*, both Mary and Abraham must continue to live in and embrace the finite and temporal world—after all, both cheerfully keep their sons—even though they also paradigmatically exemplify that the particular is higher than the universal.

And then the greatest knight of faith is introduced almost in passing, the knight of faith who is willing to turn the logic of the tragic hero on its head with the words, "Do not weep for me, but weep for yourself" (58/66).[17] This cryptic citation merely hints at the deeply paradoxical notion (with the requisite distress and anxiety) that Christ was not beholden to the ethical any more than Abraham was. Yet he loved as no one has ever loved. The ever-present danger of the suspension of the ethical, therefore, meant that one could never assume a comfortable or socially appropriate outcome from an encounter with Christ. In short, *de silentio* seems to be suggesting that the prospect of meeting Christ ought to terrify and appall one as much as one ought to be terrified and appalled at Abraham's willingness to sacrifice Isaac.[18] And with this suggestion, *de silentio* reminds his readers that Christ, as the paradoxical God-man,[19] stands above the ethical immediately before *de silentio* launches the next chapter with an attack against what he takes to be Hegel's conflation of the ethical with the divine.

17. See Luke 23:28. As is common in Kierkegaard's writings, the plural "yourselves and your children" in the biblical text is changed to the singular "yourself." The reason for this frequent shift should be self-evident by this point in *Fear and Trembling*.

18. And, for this reason, closing the chapter with a return to passion seems entirely appropriate because passion is an expression of spiritual toil.

19. See *Philosophical Fragments* and *Practice in Christianity* for Kierkegaard's fuller development of Jesus as the paradoxical God-man.

DISCUSSION QUESTIONS

1. What does *de silentio* mean by "teleological suspension of the ethical?" And, how does his use of Hegel help us understand what he means by "ethical" here?

2. *De silentio* argues that his contemporaries sought something like their salvation through the maintenance of their society. Why does he think this is problematic? Is this a temptation today?

3. Is *de silentio* then arguing for what we would understand to be generally immoral or unlawful behavior by those who have faith?

6

PROBLEM II

IN PROBLEM II, *de silentio* circles back to interrogate the role
of the ethical, *Sittlichkeit*, once again. This time, however, he
presses the question of the relationship between the ethical
and God further than in Problem I. Increasingly familiar
characters like Hegel, Agamemnon, and the knights of infinite resignation and faith reappear, while Abraham remains
the critical fulcrum around which the argument is shaped.
New targets for criticism also emerge, targets that include
biblical interpreters and groups that *de silentio* refers to as
sectarians (which are not limited to but would certainly
include those we refer to as communitarians today).

The internal structure of Problem II is looser than that
of Problem I, but the two chapters are formally quite similar
nonetheless. Problem II begins with another straightforward question: "Is there an absolute duty to God?" (59/68).
Again, the short answer is yes, in the case of Abraham there
is an absolute duty to God (61/70). In order to illuminate
(*a*) why this is the case and (*b*) how this question differs
from that found in Problem I, I will again attend to the
pivotal background premise that frames *de silentio*'s understanding of the question before turning to his response.
And, again, it is important to remember that the position

outlined at the beginning of Problem II is not Kierkegaard's point of view; it is a succinct summary of what he takes to be a Hegelian position that is challenged by *de silentio*.

≈

Up front, perhaps the best way to get a handle on the relationship between the question that opens Problem I—"Is there a teleological suspension of the ethical?" (46/54)—and the question that opens Problem II is as follows: the first question asks whether, at least in the case of Abraham, there are duties that might supersede one's duty to the ethical; the second question more specifically asks what it might mean if one's duty to God is higher than one's duty to the ethical (remembering, of course, the particular sense of the ethical that *de silentio* is referring to). There is considerable overlap here. But there are also nuances and increased specificities that slowly lead the reader to see how *de silentio*'s battle with a Hegelian point of view really matters for ordinary Christians. Before getting ahead of myself, however, unpacking the logic of the presumed Hegelian posture is necessary.

Premise: The ethical is the divine. Building on the claim that the ethical is the universal,[1] *de silentio* also claims that, as such, the ethical is "in turn the divine" (59/68). In the previous chapter, we already noticed *de silentio*'s worry that participation in the ethical has the same character as gaining eternal salvation. Here, he describes the divine nature of the universal by indicating that every duty is a duty to God and that it becomes a duty "by being referred to God" (59/68), that is, the duty can be traced back to an authority referred to as God. For example, it is a duty to love one's

1. See chapter 5.

neighbor because it is a duty that originates with God.[2] In claiming that the ethical is the divine, *de silentio* is not necessarily suggesting that people call the ethical—*Sittlichkeit*—God, or that those who are aligned with the ethical give up speaking as if there is a God other than the ethical. What *de silentio* is attempting to name is the very problematic position that lies behind the confusing God-talk that results when Christians accept that the ethical is the universal that cannot be teleologically suspended. This position and its entailments can be sketched by highlighting the corollary to the premise that the ethical is the divine.

Corollary 1: There is no duty to God. From the perspective of the Hegelian position, to speak of the ethical as universal is to refuse anything higher than the ethical since the universal applies at all times and places. Therefore, whatever attempts are made to root the ethical in God (or divine authority) fail because "God becomes an invisible vanishing point" (59/68). What *de silentio* is driving at in offering this assessment is that, according to Hegel, there is no relationship to God other than through the ethical, that one cannot love God other than through the ethical. If this is the case, then God disappears into the ethical and, in the process, the ethical becomes divinized because it functions as God. Or, to state this position negatively, God apart from the ethical is "an impotent thought" (59/68). *De silentio* playfully and poignantly suggests that, in this view, the impersonal phantom that God has become would merely say, "I do not ask for your love, just stay where you belong" (60/68).

On the contrary: Hegel is wrong! The ethical is not the divine. Again, this bold evaluation is the critical turning

2. At this level, the Hegelian point of view has vague similarities to Kant's practical reason that ultimately postulates God as a Divine Legislator. See Kant, *Critique of Practical Reason*.

point in the chapter's argument. According to *de silentio*, Hegelian philosophy, in its narration of the development of the world, positions the outer, the ethical, the concrete actualization of ethics culminating in a nation's laws as the highest form of existence. In the ethical, the individual divests herself of the qualifications of inwardness.[3] This is, as one might guess, a less than sympathetic interpretation of Hegel, who seems to want to claim that inwardness is taken up and concretized in the ethical. But *de silentio*'s point is clear: faith is paradoxically higher than the ethical because, in faith, one has an absolute duty to the absolute that relativizes—*without abolishing*—the ethical.[4] Therefore, whatever philosophical or theological system assumes a universal that cannot be relativized by one's relationship to God cannot account for Abraham's faith because his faith is paradoxically related to the ethical.

Two further clarifications are in order because *de silentio* is slowly refining what he means by inwardness. First, the inwardness of faith he is concerned with is not an "inward qualification of feeling, mood, etc." (60/69), or what Kierkegaard in other contexts will include under the umbrella of the aesthetic (71/82).[5] Rather, faith is a different kind of inwardness or immediacy that contains an absolute duty to God. Both are departures from the ethical, and for Kierkegaard, it is probably too simple but also fair to say that the former is lower than the ethical while the latter is higher than the ethical. Second, *de silentio* again

3. For Hegel, inwardness is located in the abstract stage of *Moralität* that must be expressed concretely in the ethical. See, for example, Hegel, *Elements of the Philosophy of Right*, 185–86.

4. What it means to claim that the ethical is relativized but not abolished is somewhat cryptic in *Fear and Trembling*. When examining *Works of Love* we will return to this theme more extensively.

5. See, for example, *Either/Or I* and the first part of *Stages on Life's Way* for a variety of literary depictions of the life of an aesthete.

reinforces the non-dialectical shape of faith by reiterating that there is no way to assume or manipulate a movement from the ethical to faith. The most one can—and must—do is to undertake the task of infinite resignation. This task, as Socrates illustrates, "is adequate for human strength" (61/69). But, in turning away from the finite, all one gains is exhaustion and the kind of ignorance for which Socrates has become famous.[6] In this respect, *de silentio* seems to be in agreement with Hegel's understanding of Socrates: "[Socrates] evaporated the existing world and retreated into himself in search of the right and the good."[7] In the eyes of *de silentio*, to get as far as Socrates (which is precisely as far as Descartes in a different vein) was a stunningly difficult task and exceedingly rare, especially in nineteenth-century Denmark. Yet *de silentio* also believes that faith really does lie beyond Socrates even though it cannot be strategized or conceptualized (i.e., brought into a dialectical schema). The movement of faith is, as in Problem I, to receive the non-dialectical movement of the absurd: to allow faith to "break forth," to "commence, unexpectedly" (61/69). And to the story of Abraham *de silentio* again returns to display precisely this paradox.

The remainder of the chapter, like Problem I, seeks to use more tangible means to flesh out the theoretical argument that has been developed in the opening pages of the chapter. Before turning to these, however, allow me to pause very briefly on a word of warning that will dominate the next chapter: the knight of faith must accept that she

6. See Plato's *Apology* 21d: "I am wiser than this man; for neither of us really knows anything fine and good, but this man thinks he knows something when he does not, whereas I, as I do not know anything, do not think I do either. I seem, then, in just this little thing to be wiser than this man at any rate, that what I do not know I do not think I know either."

7. Hegel, *Elements of the Philosophy of Right*, 167.

will not be understood, that she will be subject to misunderstanding, that she will have no way to explain herself. According to *de silentio*, it is important to note that a teleological suspension of the universal can all too often look like an act of "the highest egoism" (62/71), namely, that one refuses the universal for one's own sake. This is, unsurprisingly, the sort of charge Hegel levels against Socrates and the Stoics. Yet—and here is the rub—the knight of faith has no way to explain how suspending the universal for God's sake is not the same thing as acting for one's own sake in a manner that is understandable to the ethical. If faith could be mediated in the language of the universal, it would then become enveloped within the universal and therefore become annulled.

∼

In the remaining pages of the chapter, *de silentio* does not appeal primarily to literary or historical characters to illustrate his argument (though he does do this). Rather, he turns to engage and explicate what he takes to be a corresponding and equally challenging passage in the New Testament: Luke 14:26, "Whoever comes to me and does not hate father and mother, wife and children, brothers and sisters, yes, and even life itself, cannot be my disciple." This too is a "remarkable teaching on the absolute duty to God" (63/72). In order to highlight the deep parallels between the "logic" of this exhortation in the Gospel of Luke and the story of Abraham, three comments are in order.

First, *de silentio* does not back down from the language of hate any more than he backs away from describing Abraham's actions with the language of murder. He acknowledges that Luke offers a very difficult exhortation and that it will generate no small amount of distress and anxiety. He also pours scorn on the textual critics and tasteful exegetes who seek to defuse the offensiveness of the text, charging them with trying "to smuggle Christianity into the world" and thereby make Christianity lukewarm, "one of the most pitiable things in the world" (63/72).[8] No, there is no comfort here: *de silentio* demands that the fear and trembling occasioned by the text be embraced directly.

Second, it is important to note that *de silentio* has a particular or qualified understanding of hate as well. After all, Christians are called to love the neighbor and therefore they cannot hate. Or, to restate with reference to Genesis, Abraham is no Cain. So how, then, can they also be called to hate? The answer to this question lies in *de silentio*'s unfolding of love as paradoxical in relation to the world, in relation to the ethical. And this brings me to the third comment.

Finally, to hate one's parents, spouse, and siblings can be nothing other than teleologically suspending the ethical in one's duty to the absolute: "The absolute duty may then bring one to do what ethics would forbid, but it can never make the knight of faith stop loving" (65/74). Just as Abraham's actions could only be described as intent to murder by the ethical, a Christian's love may be described as hate for the same reason. But the knight of faith never ceases to love in the manner required by God even if it transgresses the ethical and is misunderstood by those who are loved.

∼

8. This is a familiar theme in Kierkegaard's later writings, and perhaps the best image he provides is found in *For Self-Examination*: the reader cunningly shoves in, "one layer after another, interpretation and scholarly research, and more scholarly research (much in the way a boy puts a napkin or more under his pants when he is going to get a licking)" (35).

To this point in *Fear and Trembling*, *de silentio* seems to have focused his critique against Christians who have embraced the state as the instantiation of the ethical, and, given the unfolding of Hegel's thought, this probably ought to be expected. In the final pages of Problem II, however, *de silentio* turns his ideological critique* against the church itself as another tempting instantiation of the ethical. It is helpful to remember that Kierkegaard was writing in the context of nineteenth-century Danish Christendom; it may also be helpful to remember that Kierkegaard understood his writings to be serving as a corrective to the excesses of his contemporary context;[9] it may also be helpful to remember that *de silentio* is not Kierkegaard.[10] That said, the logic inherent in *de silentio*'s challenge to the institutional church cannot be weakened "to a certain extent"—it is either consistent with what he has developed to this point or it is not.

> Furthermore, the passage in Luke must be understood in such a way that one perceives that the knight of faith has no higher expression of the universal (as the ethical) at all in which he can save himself. If we thus let the church require this sacrifice from one of its members, then we have only a tragic hero. For the idea of the church is not qualitatively different from that of the state, inasmuch as the single individual can enter into it by a simple mediation. Upon entering into the paradox, the single individual does not arrive at the idea of the church; he does

9. Returning to the emphasis of how over what, Kierkegaard would later state, "My task has continually been to provide the existential-corrective by poetically presenting the ideals and inciting people about the established order" (*Journals and Papers*, I 708).

10. To be sure, Kierkegaard's late "attack on Christendom" looks very much like the early critique found here. See Kierkegaard, *The Moment and Late Writings*.

not leave the paradox but must find either his eternal blessedness or his perdition within it. (65/74)

What *de silentio* is driving at here is that the church remains just as much a temptation for the knight of faith as the state, for they both assume accounts of intelligibility that can envelop—thereby nullifying—an individual's God-relationship into the universal. To give in to this temptation is to become a counterfeit knight that stands far below even the knight of infinite resignation or the tragic hero—like Agamemnon—that eventually finds rest in the universal. Both of these options merely speak of God "in the third person" (68/77) and not directly.

Those who have long rejected Christendom and celebrate our current post-Christendom context should pause before celebrating *de silentio*'s critique of the institutional church too quickly. This critique also runs deep enough to cut through what he refers to as sectarianism,* namely, "an attempt to jump off the narrow way of the paradox and become a tragic hero on the cheap" (and it is cheap because it refuses the demands of both the paradox and the universal) (69/79). In context, *de silentio* might be referring to followers of Nicolai Grundtvig,* but more likely he is referring to groups of Moravian Pietists* to which Kierkegaard had direct relationships.[11] He continues, "The sectarians deafen each other with noise and clamor, they keep anxiety away by their screaming, and a hooting menagerie such as this thinks it is storming heaven and treads the same path as the knight of faith" (70/80). What the sectarian lacks is the willingness "to endure the martyrdom of unintelligibility" (70/80). The language of martyr here is intentional because the basic charge is that the sectarian is not content to be a

11. See Barnett, *Kierkegaard, Pietism and Holiness.*

witness to faith (the definition of martyr in the Christian tradition). The sectarian wants to be affirmed by others in the world. Further, the sectarian wants to be a teacher who knows and is able to communicate faith (which is precisely, according to *de silentio*, to corrupt faith).

So what is wrong with being a teacher? For *de silentio*, the basic problem turns out to be another form of mediation, that is, the teacher self-consciously places himself between God and the learner.[12] This may be fine for mathematics and spelling. But becoming a knight of faith, an individual before God, is not something that can be learned secondhand. To presume to teach faith is, for *de silentio*, to deny the "deep humanity" that must be presumed in other people.[13] And right on cue, Problem III then turns to examine Abraham's silent witness in contrast to a variety of false analogues.

DISCUSSION QUESTIONS

1. What does *de silentio* mean when he suggests that the ethical is the divine? For whom does this description apply?

2. Why does *de silentio* appeal to inwardness in order to address the problem of God becoming what he calls a "vanishing point?" What are the unique features of this kind of inwardness?

3. What does *de silentio* mean when he asserts that to hate one's mother and father is a remarkable teaching about

12. In *Philosophical Fragments* (published a year after *Fear and Trembling*), Kierkegaard's pseudonym Johannes Climacus argues that the only teacher possible in this respect is Jesus Christ. See Kierkegaard, *Philosophical Fragments*, 14–18.

13. See, again, Kierkegaard's literary strategy of indirect communication.

the absolute duty to God? How is this assertion related
to the movements of infinite resignation and faith?

4. Today, it is common to hear critiques of Christians who
emphasize belief and seem to ignore the importance of
good works. Would these same critiques apply to the
position articulated by *de silentio*? Explain.

7

PROBLEM III

STRUCTURALLY, PROBLEM III IS asymmetrical in relation to
the two previous chapters: it is long and composed of seem-
ingly unrelated ramblings about mythical or poetic characters—peppered with various asides—that clearly do not
provide the reader with insight into Abraham's actions. In
short, one may even be tempted to imagine that *de silentio*'s
editor took a bit of a nap while he snuck this last problem
into *Fear and Trembling*. Upon closer examination, however, one may more sympathetically suspect that *de silentio* is
attempting to perform his own argument here, namely, he
is attempting to demonstrate that the whole investigation—
any investigation, even an unlimited poetic investigation
of characters and concepts—only leads to one conspicuous
conclusion: Abraham is unintelligible (99/112). That said
(and more will be said below), one can only agree with
this conclusion if *de silentio* is in fact intelligible, and I
believe he is. The task before me, therefore, is to provide
a roadmap, along with a few signposts, for the purpose of
elucidating the coherent development of Problem III, even
if that development is explicitly oriented toward deepening
the dissonance between the reader and Abraham's faith.

⤳

Initially, it seems as if we are entering familiar territory as *de silentio* begins with a question: "Was it ethically defensible for Abraham to conceal his understanding from Sarah, from Eliezer, from Isaac?" (71/82). Very quickly, however, we sense something is slightly different here. First, the answer to this question is, for the first time, stated as a negative: no, it is not ethically defensible for Abraham to do so. Second, the specific detail in the question is unique to this problem—Sarah is Abraham's wife; Eliezer, his servant; Isaac, his son. What *de silentio* seems to be highlighting here is a shift away from his critique of the state and the church (which are present in the previous problems) to Abraham's more immediate relationships, to which he ought to have ethical responsibilities. In this naming, *de silentio* shows that he is digging still deeper into Hegel's logic and tracing it all the way to the earliest forms of *Sittlichkeit*. What I mean is that *de silentio*'s advance in Problem III is a veiled attempt to follow Abraham's development back—back from his civic (and, to speak anachronistically, his national) context to the prior and first step needed to turn from inwardness to the ethical, namely, to Abraham's marriage as "the immediate ethical responsibility"[1] that then serves as the context for attributing an "ethical quality" to the family's resources (e.g., Eliezer) and the upbringing of children (e.g., Isaac), in that order.[2] These are what *de silentio* seems to be referring to as "ethical intermediary forums" (71/82).[3]

Since *de silentio* presumes familiarity with the argument of the previous problems, the logic of the position

---

1. Hegel, *Elements of the Philosophy of Right*, 200.

2. Ibid., 209–18.

3. Kierkegaard later refers to them as "three ethical agents" (*Fear and Trembling*, 99/112).

behind the question in Problem III is presented in an abbreviated fashion:

Premise: The ethical is the disclosed. By now, this aspect of the Hegelian account of the ethical has appeared numerous times. In short, the human being as "sensuous and psychical"—as feeling and thinking—is concealed, directed inward, or, to restate, is not yet actualized or concretized in the universal. To do so requires disclosure in the language of the universal, that is, the ethical. And according to *de silentio*, "The Hegelian philosophy assumes no justified concealment" (71/82).

On the contrary: Hegel is wrong! Again, we see *de silentio* claiming that the individual is higher than the universal. Yes, he acknowledges that Hegel may be right that the immediacy of the aesthetic ought to be disclosed in the ethical. Yet faith is not the aesthetic (and by aesthetic, of course, he is again referring to a particular kind of existence). Faith is a second, post-encounter-with-God immediacy and, therefore, Abraham cannot disclose his undertaking even though, according to the ethical, failure to do so is indefensible. With this, his explanation stops short.

The brevity of *de silentio*'s theoretical development of Problem III is, however, inversely proportional to the length of his illustration—what begins as "an esthetic deliberation" (72/82) quickly transitions to an examination of numerous false analogs to Abraham. Before addressing individual aspects of the remainder of the chapter, it may be helpful to see them in context. To that end, the following serves as a type of "table of contents" or map for the rest of the chapter:[4]

4. By "the rest of the chapter," I am referring to 72–106 in the Evans and Walsh edition and 82–120 in the Hong and Hong translation.

1. Introduction of "the interesting"

2. Aesthetic concealment and ethical recognition

    a. girl secretly in love

    b. *Iphigenia at Aulis*

    c. Amor and Psyche

3. Paradoxical secrecy as divine or demonic

    a. Aristotle's bridegroom in Delphi

        a.i. Axel and Valborg*

        a.ii. Queen Elizabeth and Essex*

    b. *Agnes and the Merman**

        *aside on sin

        *aside on monasticism

    c. Tobias and Sarah

        c.i. Gloucester*

        *aside on the genius

    d. *Faust**

    e. New Testament

        *aside on irony

4. Abraham

    *aside on the intellectual tragic hero

To begin to illumine Abraham negatively—that is, to illumine modes of existence that Abraham does not represent—*de silentio* introduces the category of "the interesting" (#1 above). This term, rather overused today, was newly introduced into Kierkegaard's world through the Romantics (and especially Friedrich Schlegel). For *de silentio*, the term represents an unstable category, a *confinium* or border territory between the aesthetic and the ethical. Particularly, in this context, the interesting is relevant because it is not governed by fate; it is a category where the subjective will is expressed in free action; it is a category accompanied by trouble and pain precisely because it always stands at a turning point (and Socrates is again brought forward as a noteworthy exemplar).

With reference to Aristotle's* *Poetics*, the particular turning point *de silentio* wants to draw attention to is the moment of ethical recognition (#2 above). Implied in the moment of recognition, for *de silentio*, is a prior moment of concealment (73/83) and therein lies the necessary condition for the category of the interesting. To state the obvious, what interests *de silentio* in this problem is the prospective transition from concealment to recognition. He quotes Aristotle to orient his discussion, but it is important to note that Hegel's concept of recognition—the process by which self-reflection is recognized, known, and willed, thereby mediating the individual into the universal, the ethical—haunts the entire discourse even though it is not explicitly mentioned.[5] To restate, the concealment/recognition tension here formally and materially mirrors the inner/outer tension addressed in the earlier problems. And we will soon find that aesthetic concealment parallels what he has earlier referred to as first immediacy, while faith is a qualitatively different kind of concealment. Stepping back for a moment, we can see that what *de silentio* is also doing is non-identically repeating what he did in the "Tuning Up" section at the beginning of *Fear and Trembling*—he is de-

5. Although recognition plays a significant role in the development of Hegel's *Phenomenology of Spirit* (111ff.), it appears precisely as one would expect it in *Elements of the Philosophy of Right* as well: "But it is this very sphere of relativity . . . [the administration of justice] . . . which gives right an *existence* in which it is *universally recognized, known,* and *willed,* and in which, through the mediation of this quality of being known and willed, it has validity and objective actuality" (240, emphasis in original).

picting possible ways to comprehend the story of Abraham, none of which is compatible with the claim that Abraham is the father of faith (which we will see when he finally arrives at #4 above).

The particularities of Problem III deserve much more attention than can be afforded in this small volume. However, two comments on the relationship between concealment and recognition are in order before moving to the specific examples. First, *de silentio* distinguishes between Greek and modern tragedy—the former is driven by fate (and therefore is not interesting), while the latter is "sighted, introspective, [and] assimilates fate into its dramatic consciousness" (73/84).[6] Or, the modern hero is capable of subjectivity; in this way, the modern hero is responsible in a way that is foreign to Greek tragedy. Second, *de silentio* is not interested in the concealment of nonsense, that is, the sort of concealment that has nothing to do with the universal or the idea. That sort of concealment is the province of comedy, and perhaps more accurately, farce.[7]

To highlight the contest between aesthetic concealment and the ethical, *de silentio* provides three examples. The first—that of a girl secretly in love—is presented to indicate that aesthetic concealment is resolved aesthetically outside of time (happily ever after, if you will) but, if it is to be fulfilled in time, it must be disclosed or punished by ethics. The second—drawn from *Iphigenia at Aulis*—confirms

6. This is not the first time in Kierkegaard's corpus that the contrast between modern and ancient tragedy is raised. For an earlier examination from the perspective of a different pseudonym, see *Either/Or I*, 137–63.

7. Kierkegaard also distinguishes humor from comedy, and he has much to say about humor that is salutary and theologically useful. See, for example, Lippitt, *Humour and Irony in Kierkegaard's Thought*. Further, for a series of pseudonymous comments on farce published the same year as *Fear and Trembling*, see *Repetition*, 158–66.

that aesthetics itself may also demand disclosure, but it must utilize coincidence or some other aesthetic ruse (since, for *de silentio*, the aesthetic has no inherent logic that necessarily ends in the ethical). Further, it also confirms that the tragic hero does not belong to the aesthetic but to the ethical, for he satisfies the demand for disclosure supremely. Third and finally, Amor and Psyche* appear as *de silentio* begins to transition to the next section. They are drawn forward to demonstrate that secrecy and silence are not signs of weakness but rather are signs of greatness "precisely because they are qualifications of inwardness" (77/88).

But again, not all qualifications of inwardness are equal, not even all of those that do not fall into the category of aesthetic concealment. What I mean is that, once *de silentio* has established that aesthetic concealment is unstable and untenable in time, he turns his attention to a contrast that becomes visible for the first time—the contrast between demonic and divine secrecy (#3 above). Both stand beyond the ethical, the "purely human" (77/88); both are paradoxical; both are silent. Immediately, *de silentio* jumps into examples.

The first example provided by *de silentio* is taken from the pages of Aristotle's *Politics*: a bridegroom, as he is about to "fetch his bride," receives a prediction from an augur that a misfortune arising from his marriage will befall him (78/89). It is a sad tale to be sure, but two elements of the story are essential for *de silentio*—the story takes place in ancient Greece and the pronouncement of misfortune is a divine pronouncement (and not the bridegroom's imagination or wish). After the prediction, the bridegroom has three possible responses: (1) he can keep silent and get married, (2) he can keep silent and not get married, or (3) he can speak. The bridegroom is a hero, however, and therefore must necessarily choose the last option. He must speak even if the whole affair then becomes "an unhappy love story" (80/91):[8] "His heroism consists essentially, then, in giving up the esthetic high-mindedness" (80/92). Even though *de silentio* still gets no further than displaying a tragic hero, the sketch is useful because it can be used to cast light on the paradox that he has been pointing to since the beginning of *Fear and Trembling*. He does so by reimagining the story beyond its original context. The Greek context is problematic for *de silentio*'s purposes: the augur is a publicly acceptable feature of Greek political life that speaks in a manner that is intelligible to all and is also a predictor of fate that cannot be altered by the bridegroom. Therefore, there is no hiddenness in the augur's prediction and there is certainly nothing that the bridegroom can do to "come into closer relation to the divine or become an object either of its grace or of its wrath" (81/93). But then *de silentio* states, "If heaven's will had not been proclaimed to him by an augur, if it had been brought to his knowledge quite privately, if it had placed itself in an altogether private relationship to him, then we are at the paradox, if, that is, it exists" (81/93). Then the bridegroom could find himself with the conditions for an absolute relationship to the absolute. Then the bridegroom could find a kind of rest beyond the ethical in the religious, "for this power is the only one that can rescue the esthetic from its combat with the ethical" (82/93).[9]

Having elaborately set the stage for the purpose of introducing the religious (again, we are speaking of a way

8. It is in this context that *de silentio* introduces the comparison with Axel and Valborg, another mythical couple separated by heaven (though they were separated for a specific reason) (80/91–92).

9. *De silentio* then introduces a brief summary of Queen Elizabeth's love for Essex that was heroically sacrificed to the state and her subsequent silence unto death—another expression of the transition from the aesthetic to the ethical that shatters the aesthetic "illusions of magnanimity" in silence (82/93).

of existing or stage of existence), *de silentio* then turns to address the demonic directly. There are multiple layers in *de silentio*'s development of the legend of Agnes and the merman, and he introduces new ones with every variation to the story. First, *de silentio* presents a version of the story in which the merman is a seducer—the merman attempts to seduce Agnes and, just before diving into the sea with her in his arms, Agnes's innocence disarms him.[10] Recognizing that Agnes cannot be seduced, he takes her back to her home. In this version of the story, the merman simply loses Agnes and returns to the sea in wild despair. I will return to the merman's despair shortly but, before doing so, let us move to the second variation in which the merman is given a human conscience (subjectivity) and a human pre-existence (temporality). With these, he is no longer an imaginary phantom merely driven by lust; the merman is equipped to become a hero, or to rephrase, the merman is equipped to become ethical. He is, therefore, forced to make a choice between the following: (1) repentance of his attempted seduction of Agnes, or (2) Agnes *and* repentance of his attempted seduction (84/96). The former is an act that occurs in silence; the latter provides a way into the ethical through marriage.

With this choice, *de silentio* raises the stakes and begins to unfold the essential difference between the demonic in relation to the knight of faith. Repentance, taken by

10. *De silentio*, despite the fact that his focus is on the merman, and almost as an aside, turns his attention to Agnes in order to comment on "modernized" women and their penchant for "the interesting" (83/95). Here, and in his later unflattering comment on women—equating women with the uneducated (88/101)—Kierkegaard reflects many of the problematic patriarchal assumptions and practices of his time. For a good place to begin critically examining this aspect of his thought, see Léon and Walsh, *Feminist Interpretations of Søren Kierkegaard.*

itself, is a human process much like infinite resignation. In repentance, the merman gives up what he has acquired—Agnes—in the world. He may love Agnes, but he acknowledges that his acquisitive seduction is at odds with this love. Therefore, he must repent of the guilt he has also acquired in his seduction. But how is the merman to repent? On one hand, he can use the demonic. What *de silentio* means here is that there is a sense in which the merman can use the demonic element to ensure that Agnes gives up her love for him, thereby saving herself (and in a surprising comment, *de silentio* suggests that there is infinitely more goodness in a demoniac than in shallow people) (84/96).[11] The demonic—shocking terminology for some in our contemporary context—does not receive systematic treatment here, but it seems to refer to something like consistent self-directed inwardness or, stated most strongly, an absolute relationship to oneself (which is one way to understand *de silentio*'s acknowledgment that one can enter into an absolute relation to the demonic). Of note, the language employed by *de silentio* is framed in terms of psychology and not dogmatics, much like the argument of *The Concept of Anxiety*, published by Kierkegaard a year later under the pseudonym Vigilius Haufniensis. The demonic, nonetheless, is the means by which the merman is a single individual "who as the particular was higher than the universal" (85/97). One should also remember that the demoniac, understood this way, is formally similar and yet the opposite of the state of having an absolute relation to the absolute.

The merman therefore is not Abraham. The merman merely stands at a "dialectical apex" (85/98) in which two

11. Commentators have often understood at least this section of *Fear and Trembling* to resonate with Kierkegaard's own relationship with Regine Olsen, since Kierkegaard did attempt something like this after formally breaking off their engagement.

paths are possible if the merman is to be rescued from the demonic (remembering, of course, that this fork in the road is subsequent to the earlier choice of repentance vs. Agnes *and* repentance). Yet, both of the paths out of the demonic depend on the divine: (1) the merman remains in concealment and finds rest in the "counter-paradox" (85/98) that the divine will save Agnes; or (2) the merman is saved for temporality through marriage to Agnes. For *de silentio* (and for Kierkegaard), medieval monastic life exemplifies this first path excellently, and this is not exactly a compliment for the simple reason that the monk, like the knight of infinite resignation, would still not have made the movement of the absurd, the movement of faith, the joyful reception of temporality.[12] The second path is even more complicated for reasons that *de silentio* is unqualified to discuss with any authority: "For when the single individual by his guilt has come outside the universal, he can only return to it by virtue of having come as the single individual into an absolute relation to the absolute" (86/98).

When we reach the limits of *de silentio*'s poetic license, however, we have not yet reached the limits of one of Kierkegaard's central concerns, namely, sin.[13] Like faith, sin is

12. Although *de silentio* believes the monastic life to be incomplete, it is still an example of a rigorous examined life—parallel to Socrates in almost every way—that has gone much further than the Christianity of nineteenth-century Denmark: "And yet what higher movement has the age discovered since the day it gave up entering the monastery? Is it not a wretched worldly wisdom, prudence, cowardice that sits in the place of honor, cravenly dupes people into thinking they have attained the highest?" (88/100).

13. The footnote at the bottom of page 86/98 is very helpful for understanding the limits of *de silentio*'s perspective: once Christian dogmatic categories are introduced, the entire conversation changes. What Kierkegaard is attempting with *de silentio* is to see how far one can go in speaking about Abraham's faith before these dogmatic categories need to be introduced. Of course, the fact that sin is introduced

a second immediacy; like faith, sin can only exist once one is personally related to God. Guilt is not sin, but guilt and despair (psychologically understood) are on the way to sin. In *Sickness unto Death*, Kierkegaard's late pseudonym Anti-Climacus states this as follows: "To sin is: 'after being taught by a revelation from God what sin is, before God in despair not to will to be oneself or in despair to will to be oneself.'"[14] Or, to use the categories of *Fear and Trembling*, to sin is to choose the demonic instead of an absolute relation to the absolute once one is aware that one has to choose between the two.[15] "Before God" is the critical element that makes sin possible, yet it is only "before God" that the merman encounters the possibility of reconciliation with temporality, with Agnes. To choose oneself over an absolute relation to the absolute is to become a demoniac, which is essentially self-destruction (86–87/99). But Abraham is not the merman. The merman breaks from the universal through his guilt (that is, his desire to seduce Agnes). Abraham breaks from the universal without incurring guilt. Yet, both must return to temporality through the absurd, through the paradoxical absolute relation to the absolute.

---

suggests that *Fear and Trembling* actually cannot be understood apart from reference to Christian categories (or at least their qualitative limits), though there is considerable debate in scholarly circles about just how much Christian categories inform the text.

This is, of course, to also say that *de silentio* assumes the earlier reference to sin (in Problem I) as the assertion of particularity against the universal in Hegelian philosophy falls short of what Christian dogmatics refers to as sin.

14. Kierkegaard, *Sickness unto Death*, 101.

15. Again, a glance at *Sickness unto Death* helps describe what is at stake already in *Fear and Trembling*. In the opening pages of *Sickness unto Death*, Anti-Climacus describes a "self": ultimately, the self can only find rest and equilibrium in relating itself to "that which has established the entire relation," namely, God (14).

Having established the difference between the mer-man and Abraham in terms of how they broke from the universal, *de silentio* introduces another romantic pairing, drawn from the book of Tobit: Tobias and Sarah. In their story, Sarah has been married seven times and, each time, her would-be husband has perished in the bridal chamber. Then Tobias wants to marry Sarah. Refusing to focus on the chivalry of Tobias, *de silentio* lets the accent fall on Sarah, the one he describes as "more unhappy than anyone, for she knows that the evil demon who loves her will kill the bridegroom on the wedding night" (89/102). While he spends several pages developing this heart-rending story from various directions, *de silentio*'s central driving point is to illustrate that, in the case of Sarah, it is simply foolish to demand—as the ethical does—that she should express the universal and get married. It is not possible. Or, to state his point another way: some are placed outside the univer-sal "by nature or historical circumstance"—whether they be Shakespeare's Gloucester or a great genius[16]—in such a way that they cannot be mediated into the idea of society (93/106). All of these supplementary examples serve *de silentio* by demonstrating even further possibilities for rela-tivizing the ultimacy of the universal: being placed outside the universal is the beginning of the demonic without the merman's incursion of guilt.[17] It does not determine one's

16. Speaking of the category of genius, Kierkegaard's most fa-mous treatment of the genius and her eventual sublation into society can be found in a small essay titled "The Difference between a Genius and an Apostle," published pseudonymously by H. H. in 1847. See Kierkegaard, *Without Authority*, 91–108.

17. It is also important to note that *de silentio* continues his de-velopment of the demonic by imagining Sarah as a man: "Let Sarah be a man and the demonic is immediately at hand" (91/104). In this context, Gloucester, too, is portrayed as a vile demoniac that is even-tually lost in the demonic paradox.

final relationship to either the absolute or the ethical—and one can assume the subsequent possible paths available in this context are the same as those available to the merman—but it does determine a starting point outside the universal that cannot be ignored. But again, none of these examples are Abraham because Abraham is already happily married with an heir before he is called to sacrifice Isaac.

Finally, before returning to Abraham, *de silentio* turns to Faust. Again, the Faust legend has a rich and diverse history that Kierkegaard has already engaged for different purposes in *Either/Or I*. In this context, *de silentio* utilizes his idiosyncratic Faust by taking up a few threads already examined—especially the negative role of doubt—and casting him in such a way that he serves as a rough secular parallel to the monastic life. According to *de silentio*, Faust is ideal; he has made the movement into the world of spirit. Having done so (and because he is a doubter par excellence), he has the capacity "to frighten people into being terror-stricken, to make the ground seem to give way under their feet, to scatter people, to cause a cry of alarm to sound everywhere" (96/109). Yet, because he pities the universal, he keeps silent and remains concealed in "infinite passion" (97/110). In this form of concealment, Faust sacrifices himself to the universal without challenging it. Again, *de silentio* employs this version of Faust against his contemporaries—the "low-comedy fools in our age who run after doubt, produce an external argument, for example a doctoral certificate, to prove they really have doubted" (97/110)—in order to reinforce how difficult it is to really break from the universal without external justification or authority. But, most importantly for the movement of the chapter, Faust serves as the premier example of a magnanimous self-appointed break from the universal, a break with the universal that refuses to undermine it. What Faust lacks, however, is authorization for his silence, and here is the critical final turning point in Problem III—the turn to Abraham (#4 above).

Between Faust and Abraham, however, *de silentio* inserts a small but important paragraph concerning the New Testament. In short, he is attempting to demonstrate that even the New Testament approves of silence and irony as the means to conceal something better. Citing Matthew 6:17–18, "When you fast, anoint your head and wash your face, that people will not see you fasting" (98/111), *de silentio* concludes, "This passage testifies directly to the fact that subjectivity is incommensurable with actuality, even that it has a right to deceive" (98/111–12). These are fighting words, and a more direct attack on his contemporaries and their Hegelian theology (and Hegel is again identified specifically in this paragraph) is hard to imagine. And, having cited New Testament authorization for concealment, *de silentio* then returns to Abraham.

Finally, after what might seem like a long walk through a dark labyrinth, *de silentio* comes around to stating his purpose thus far in Problem III: "None of the stages described contained an analogy to Abraham; they were only developed in order that, while being shown within their own spheres, they could indicate, so to speak, the boundary of the unknown region at the point of variation" (99/112). No, Abraham is not a demoniac; he is not an aesthetic hero; he is not a tragic hero. No, he *cannot* speak, a refrain repeated at least three times in this final section (100/113, 101/115, and 104/118).

As it turns out, Abraham can actually use words and it is written that, when Isaac asks about the lamb for the burnt offering he is about to sacrifice, Abraham responds by saying, "God himself will provide the lamb for the burnt offering" (102/116).[18] So what does it mean, then, when *de silentio* claims that Abraham cannot speak? First, *de silentio* uses this refrain to emphasize the frightful responsibility and distress of solitude, a responsibility that far outweighs that of a tragic hero. Second, he seeks to demonstrate that Abraham's silence was oriented toward spirit and, therefore, what little he does say is merely a fulfillment of his existence with respect to spirit; that is, it is utterly unintelligible and concealed. This is, according to *de silentio*, quite the opposite of the final remarks of the intellectual tragic hero (like Socrates) who, even though oriented to spirit, provides a final comment that understandably sums up his life. Rather, Abraham's comment to Isaac has the form of irony, "for it is irony when I say something and yet do not say anything" (105/118). He does not lie, but he does not say anything that *de silentio* or the universal can understand.[19] And here lies one of the basic issues at stake in *Fear and Trembling*: talk about one's personal relationship with God is talk in "a foreign tongue" (105/119). It is not talk that can be "understood" any more than subjectivity can be commensurate with actuality. And what did Abraham achieve in his concealment? "He remained true to his love" (106/120). He refused to give in to the temptation of the universal and trade his love of God for understanding. And, in a moment in which Kierkegaard bursts through the pseudonym, the authority of the New Testament again creeps in with the affirmation of God's response: "for he sees in secret and knows the distress and counts the tears and forgets

18. See Gen 22:8.

19. *De silentio* provides another example of this sort of statement with reference to Pythagoras. When Pythagoras is condemned to death, he breaks his silence to say, "It is better to be killed than to speak" (104/118).

nothing" (106/120).[20] This is the only consolation offered to the knight of faith. And if this is not enough, Abraham cannot be the father of faith. With that stark conclusion, *de silentio* also ends Problem III.

DISCUSSION QUESTIONS

1. Why is it necessary that Abraham cannot explain his actions to his family and others? How is this point essential for understanding Abraham as a knight of faith?

2. Is it becoming even clearer why Kierkegaard chose the pseudonym Johannes *de silentio* by this point? Explain.

3. By the end of this chapter, *de silentio* is led to introduce sin. Why? He then defers addressing the concept of sin to a dogmatic context. Again, why does he do this?

4. St. Francis is credited with the following proclamation: "Preach the gospel and when necessary use words." How is this statement similar and different in relation to what *de silentio* is getting at in this chapter?

20. See Matt 6:4, 18.

8

EPILOGUE

THE FINAL RHETORICAL COMPONENT of *Fear and Trembling* is a short Epilogue that is one further performance of its argument. Immediately, *de silentio* loops back to the critical opening line of the Preface—the "veritable clearance sale" in the realm of ideas (3). He begins with a legend of a time in Holland when the price of spices was sufficiently low that merchants were willing to take the drastic action of dumping a few loads at sea to increase the demand and therefore raise the price. Without pushing the metaphor too far, this is the task of *Fear and Trembling*: to raise the price of faith. What Kierkegaard understands as the veritable clearance sale on faith is captured well in his journals:

> What Schleiermacher calls "religion" and the Hegelian dogmaticians "faith" is, after all, nothing else than the first immediacy, the pre-requisite for everything—the vital fluid—in an emotional-intellectual sense the atmosphere we breathe—and which therefore cannot properly be characterized with these words.[1]

1. Kierkegaard, *Journals and Papers*, II 1096.

No, for Kierkegaard, faith, as a *passion*, requires an expression of will.[2] It is not the first immediacy. It is a passion that is both gift and task that must be received and learned individually as a second immediacy. In *Fear and Trembling*, *de silentio* is concerned primarily with the approach to faith, with ensuring that there is no transition to faith "as a matter of course," no transition that does not relativize what is universally accepted. It is a matter of fear and trembling. Taking a shot at a Hegelian notion of the unfolding of Spirit in history, *de silentio* again asserts—as in the opening pages—that one cannot rest on the shoulders of prior generations; each generation must begin again from the beginning, and each individual must keep her hand to the plow, so to speak, for her entire life, "for the task is always sufficient for a lifetime" (108/122).

Faith is therefore also *the highest* in a human being. In a penultimate dig at his contemporary Hegelians, *de silentio* implicitly challenges the primacy of thought, of knowledge, of what Hegel would call "Absolute Knowing"—Spirit returning to itself in "the long procession of historical cultures and individuals."[3] No, universal knowledge is but a temptation and false comfort because the restlessness of faith can only find comfort in an absolute relation to the absolute.[4]

In conclusion, *de silentio* offers one final cryptic parting shot. To go further than faith is something *de silentio* has openly criticized right from the start. In fact, to go further than Socrates (who is not yet a knight of faith) is virtually unimaginable in this text. Once again, this theme is raised with reference to Heraclitus.* Briefly, Heraclitus, a pre-Socratic philosopher, observed that one cannot step

2. See ibid., 1094.

3. See Hegel, *Phenomenology of Spirit*, 591.

4. For a much fuller development of faith in *Fear and Trembling*, see Westphal, *Kierkegaard's Concept of Faith*.

into the same river twice. What he seems to have meant is that, because a river continually flows, the river never remains static. Therefore, one can never step into the same river twice because the river as it was when you first put your foot in has already flowed away (109/123). Given all that *de silentio* has said about inwardness and breaking from the universal, one can see how this basic thesis could analogously point in the direction of particularity and individuality despite the appearance of similitude. Might it be possible to go further than this? *De silentio* mockingly suggests not: at least according to the Eleatic* thesis, to go further is to refuse to move at all. Or, to go further is to deny motion, and this sounds very much like the charge *de silentio* has leveled against his Danish contemporaries: they claim to have gone further than Abraham's act of faith, but they have not even started down the path of infinite resignation. Unlike the legendary situation in Holland, however, the difficulty of faith does not need to be artificially inflated, even if some ships—false understandings of faith—need to be sunk. Rather, in *de silentio*'s words, his generation needs a "rather honest earnestness that fearlessly and incorruptibly calls attention to the tasks, an honest earnestness that lovingly preserves the tasks" (107/121). Far too simply, that is the intricate performance attempted by Kierkegaard through *de silentio* in *Fear and Trembling*.

DISCUSSION QUESTIONS

1. Why does *de silentio* return to economic metaphors or the language of exchange at this point? Or, explain why these notions have been at the center of the text's argument throughout even though not always explicitly noted.

2. What does it mean that faith is a passion? Is *de silentio* falling into a kind of aesthetic Christianity?

3. *De silentio* drives the point that faith is a task for a whole lifetime. Why do you think it is so hard for Christians to be satisfied with faith?

9

CONCLUSION

HAVING WORKED THROUGH *FEAR and Trembling* in its entirety, I hope it is at least becoming clear why Kierkegaard has been such an influential and yet enigmatic thinker in philosophical, political, and theological circles. His incisive polemics and passionate portrayals ignite the mind and stir the heart. A pedestrian companion of this sort is already at a profound disadvantage because it seeks to make plain what has been made translucent intentionally; it serves the austere purpose of attempting to clarify what probably should not need to be clarified or what probably cannot be clarified. And further, it serves as a bulky intermediary in matters where Kierkegaard sought to conceal his own role as midwife. Well, so be it—"Let anyone with ears to hear listen!"[1]

I have sought to provide a sympathetic reading of *Fear and Trembling* that uses Kierkegaard's historical and intellectual context to make some sense of the many idiosyncratic rhetorical and intellectual aspects of the text.[2] To

1. See Mark 4:9.

2. Concurrently, I have virtually ignored the reception history of the text.

this end, I have sought to shed some light on the manifold and what I take to be fundamentally orienting appearances of Hegel or Hegelian philosophy throughout the text.[3] Not all agree with me on this (and some will just be sick of the continued return to Hegel), but I am convinced that without attending to these appearances in a serious manner, *de silentio*'s text becomes much less coherent. Of course, it is necessary to note that I have made no attempt to be fair to Hegel or Hegelian philosophers here (whether nineteenth-century Danes or contemporary Hegelians)—I have merely sought to clarify *de silentio*'s interpretation of and dependence upon Hegel in this text. Therefore, it would be a serious mistake to assume without further examination that *de silentio*'s interpretation of Hegel is irrefutable or that one adequately understands Hegel or Hegelian philosophy on the basis of reading *Fear and Trembling*. Relatedly, because *Fear and Trembling* is intricately related to a program of correcting aspects of nineteenth-century Danish Christendom, to imagine that Kierkegaard is speaking directly to the early twenty-first century would require exactly that—considerable imagination. In Kierkegaardian terms, however, that is not a critique but a challenge and exhortation.[4]

Further, it is important to remember that *Fear and Trembling* provides merely one glimpse into Kierkegaard's thought. It is a revealing and riveting glimpse, but it in no way captures the breadth and depth of his Christian discourses, to say nothing about his many other pseudonymous texts. For example, if one wonders what else

3. Of course, that is not to say that *de silentio*'s critique of the ethical is limited to Hegel or Hegelians; it is to say that whatever import it has for Kant, for example, is secondary and indirect as Kant is mediated through Hegel's thought.

4. One good example of this (that reaches well beyond *Fear and Trembling*) is Kyle Roberts' *Emerging Prophet: Kierkegaard and the Postmodern People of God*.

Kierkegaard might say about attempting to step into the same river twice, I recommend continuing with *Repetition*, also published in 1843, under the pseudonym Constantin Constantius (and this name itself is a provocative witticism of sorts). Or, in another direction, much of what is left unsaid about the absurd movement of (or perhaps to) faith in *Fear and Trembling* is taken up again a year later by another pseudonym—Johannes Climacus—in *Philosophical Fragments* . . . which is then followed by a huge postscript—aptly entitled *Concluding Unscientific Postscript to Philosophical Fragments*—in 1846. As it turns out, *Fear and Trembling* is more than a celebrated text; it is an entrée into a vibrant and polyphonic corpus that is nearly as restless as the faith it commends.[5]

∽

After the publication of *Concluding Unscientific Postscript* in 1846, it seems that Kierkegaard intended to stop writing and become a pastor. In his appended "A First and Last Explanation" to *Concluding Unscientific Postscript*, Kierkegaard publicly acknowledged the by then open secret that he was the author of his pseudonymous writings. He takes the opportunity to give thanks to Governance who "has granted me much more than I had ever expected" and who "in such multitudinous ways has encouraged my endeavor."[6] He also takes a moment to thank his deceased father, "the man to whom I owe most of all."[7] And then he provides a final comment on his pseudonyms:

> With this I take leave of the pseudonymous authors with doubtful good wishes for their future

5. For a complete list of Kierkegaard's early texts, see the appendix.

6. Kierkegaard, *Concluding Unscientific Postscript I*, 628.

7. Ibid., 629.

fate, that this, if it is propitious to them, will be just as they might wish. Of course, I know them from intimate association; I know they could not expect or desire many readers—would that they might happily find the few desirable readers.

Of my reader, if I dare to speak to such a one, I would in passing request for myself a forgetful remembrance, a sign that it is of me that he is reminded, because he remembers me as irrelevant to the books, as the relationship requires, just as the appreciation for it is sincerely offered here in the moment of farewell, when I also cordially thank everyone who has kept silent and with profound veneration thank the firm Kts[8]—that it has spoken.

The "forgetful remembrance" Kierkegaard spoke of in 1846 was short-lived. In March 1847 he published the lengthy *Upbuilding Discourses in Various Spirits* (which includes the well-known discourse usually referred to as "Purity of Heart"), followed a few months later by *Works of Love* in September—both published in his own name. These first post-1846 writings thereby energetically announce what is commonly referred to as Kierkegaard's second authorship. The tenor of the authorship is no less earnest and challenging, but a transition is made to what Kierkegaard refers to as a "series of exclusively religious books,"[9] a series that would eventually also include his well-known *Sickness unto Death*, *Practice in Christianity*, *For Self-Examination*, and what has become known as the "Attack on Christendom."

8. Kts is a reference to Jakob Peter Mynster,* the long-serving bishop of Zealand to whom Kierkegaard was an ambivalent confidant. This relationship becomes considerably strained as Kierkegaard's corpus develops, though Kierkegaard, out of respect, attempted to withhold a direct attack on the Danish Church until Mynster passed away in 1854.

9. Kierkegaard, *Point of View*, 63.

The second volume in this Reading Kierkegaard miniseries turns specifically to *Works of Love*, examining it closely on its own terms much like this volume has attempted with *Fear and Trembling*. However, its secondary purposes are also to illuminate why Kierkegaard turns to "exclusively religious books" and how the second authorship reflects a self-conscious rootedness in the Christian tradition that follows from the pseudonymous texts *uno tenore*, "in one breath," as Kierkegaard would say.[10] Kierkegaard has come a long way to pose the issue of "becoming a Christian,"[11] but the time has come to tackle it directly.

DISCUSSION QUESTIONS

1. Given what you have read, do you think *de silentio* would write the same book to contemporary Christians? Why or why not?

2. At the end of the day, what about *de silentio* are we, as readers, supposed to remember? And, if *de silentio* is supposed to function as the vanishing point in the book, who or what are we, as readers, supposed to encounter in the course of reading?

10. Ibid., 6.
11. Ibid., 63.

Appendix

KIERKEGAARD'S [FIRST] AUTHORSHIP, 1841–46

Date	Title	Author/Editor
1841		
September 29	*The Concept of Irony* (Dissertation)	Kierkegaard
1843		
February 20	*Either/Or, I-II*	Victor Eremita (editor)
May 16	*Two Upbuilding Discourses*	Kierkegaard
October 16	*Fear and Trembling*	Johannes *de silentio*
October 16	*Repetition*	Constantin Constantius
October 16	*Three Upbuilding Discourses*	Kierkegaard
December 6	*Four Upbuilding Discoureses*	Kierkegaard
1844		
March 5	*Two Upbuilding Discourses*	Kierkegaard
June 13	*Philosophical Fragments*	Johannes Climacus

June 8	*Three Upbuilding Discourses*	Kierkegaard
June 17	*The Concept of Anxiety*	Vigilius Haufniensis
June 17	*Prefaces*	Nicolaus Notabene
August 31	*Four Upbuilding Discourses*	Kierkegaard

1845

April 29	*Three Discourses on Imagined Occasions*	Kierkegaard
April 30	*Stages on Life's Way*	Hilarius Bookbinder (editor)
May 19–20	"A Cursory Observation Concerning a Detail in *Don Giovanni*"	Inter et Inter

1846

| February 28 | *Concluding Unscientific Postscript* | Johannes Climacus, edited by S. Kierkegaard |
| March 30 | *Two Ages: A Literary Review* | Kierkegaard |

GLOSSARY

absurd. The absurd is a break from rational laws. This may be an event that has no obvious causal precedents or, on a more personal level, an action one feels impelled to undertake that cannot be rationally justified. It may also simply refer to a belief or hope that is held but that exceeds the bounds of reasonable calculation. This term came to be identified with Kierkegaard's thought more broadly in post-World War II French existentialism.

aesthetic (the aesthetic). The aesthetic is the first of three "spheres" in Kierkegaard's dialectical stages of existence. Life in the aesthetic sphere is marked by the cultivation of sensual experiences. The aesthete has not reached what Kierkegaard refers to as the ethical or the religious stages, and so his life is solely concerned with the fulfillment of desire.

Agamemnon. King of Argos and commander of the Greek forces during the Trojan War, Agamemnon sacrificed his daughter Iphigenia in order to secure a beneficial wind as the Greek troops set sail for Troy. Aside from his role in Euripides' *Iphigenia at Aulis* (which is taken up in *Fear and Trembling*), he features as a prominent character in Homer's *Iliad*, Aeschylus' *Oresteia*, and Euripides' *Iphigenia in Tauris*.

Agnes and the Merman. Based on an old Danish ballad, this story finds its first popular modern form in a tale by

Jens Baggesen (1764–1826); it also received treatments from Danish literary luminaries Adam Oehlenschläger (1779–1850), Christian Molbech (1783–1857), and Hans Christian Andersen (1805–75). The tale is told in many different ways but always involves a powerful merman rising out of the sea to capture and possess the beautiful maiden Agnes.

Amor and Psyche. Also known as Cupid and Psyche or Eros and Psyche, the fortunes of this pair are presented in the *Metamorphoses* or *Golden Ass* of Apuleius, a second-century CE North African sophist and writer. In short, Amor and Psyche must overcome many obstacles before they are finally united in a happy and sacred marriage.

Aristotle (384–322 BCE). A Greek philosopher and student of Plato who articulated an approach to knowledge that attempted to describe the world as it appears. In addition to serving as a teacher to Alexander the Great, Aristotle wrote on various topics including the natural world, ethics, politics, physics, rhetoric, and poetics.

Axel and Valborg. Two legendary lovers who were cousins and thus had difficulty getting permission to be married. The couple were granted a dispensation from the pope to do so, but when it was discovered that they were not only cousins but baptismal brother and sister—baptized in the same church on the same day—the marriage was ultimately prevented. Adam Oehlenschläger (1779–1850), in a five-act tragedy bearing the couple's name, made the story famous in Kierkegaard's day.

Bonhoeffer, Dietrich (1906–45). Bonhoeffer was a German pastor and theologian, and a member of the Confessing

Church. During the height of the Nazi regime, Bonhoeffer ran an underground seminary in Finkenwalde (in present-day Poland) to train pastors to nonviolently resist the German churches' embrace of fascism. In 1943, he was arrested by the Gestapo for his participation in a plot to assassinate Hitler; he was subsequently executed in 1945. Among his many writings are *Life Together*, *Discipleship*, and his *Letters and Papers from Prison*.

Brutus (d. 509 BCE). Not to be confused with Marcus Junius Brutus (a much later politician involved in the assassination of Caesar), Lucius Junius Brutus founded the Roman Republic after leading the revolt that led to the demise of Rome's last king, Lucius Tarquinius Superbus. After Brutus made the people take an oath that they would never again allow a king to rule, his two sons were involved in a plot to reinstate the Tarquin dynasty. Brutus watched as his two sons were put to death for their participation in the conspiracy.

Christendom. The Lutheran church in the Denmark of Kierkegaard's time was financially supported by the Danish state. This is the basis of the unity of church and state, such that being Danish and being a Lutheran Christian were virtually one and the same (even though church membership became voluntary after 1848). This unity of church and state known as Christendom was the object of considerable invective flowing from Kierkegaard's pen, especially late in his life.

Descartes, René (1596–1650). Descartes is widely recognized today as the "father of modern philosophy." The central goal of Descartes' philosophy was to overcome skepticism through doubt. By beginning with doubt, Descartes locates the one thing he thinks cannot be doubted: that he is doubting (which is an act of thinking). Thus, Descartes' famous *cogito ergo sum*—"I think, therefore I am"—is his rebuttal to skepticism, and it set the stage for the modern elevation of reason and thought.

dialectic (dialectical). Dialectic is a key component of logic wherein two (or more) competing positions are intrinsically related to one another. Hegel develops this concept to explain the movement of history through its various stages as a *necessary* outcome of dialectical logic. Hegel's dialectic attempts to show how history is not a simple progression forward, but each stage of history negates and overcomes its precursor. In this struggle a new stage arises and the progressive struggle begins again. For Hegel, by necessity, the further along one is in history the closer one gets to God.

Eleatics. A school of pre-Socratic Greek philosophy founded by Parmenides in the early fifth century BCE. In contrast to Heraclitus, Parmenides and the rest of the Eleatic school held that reality is always stable; change itself is a contradictory notion, and thus our empirical perception of reality as flux is a result of our faulty sensory apparatus. This position leads to the Eleatic denial of the reality of motion, referenced by Kierkegaard in both *Fear and Trembling* and *Repetition*.

Enlightenment. The Enlightenment, or what has sometimes been called the Age of Reason, is a general reference to the philosophical movement that began in the eighteenth century. The hallmark of Enlightenment philosophy is the quest for knowledge through the use of human reason. Enlightenment philosophers were largely skeptical of any kind of knowledge that could not be proven by reason, making religion based on revelation suspect.

Essex. In *Fear and Trembling,* "Essex" refers to Robert Devereux, who was the second Earl of Essex. Devereux was favored by Queen Elizabeth I, but she still allowed his execution after he was found guilty of treason.

eternity. Eternity is God's time, and as such it is separate from everyday life and its concerns. For Kierkegaard, death and entrance into eternity are certainly connected; however, one can also encounter eternity in the present life, through faith or an encounter with the God-man, Jesus Christ. Further, for Kierkegaard, eternity is understood to be qualitatively different from temporality.

existentialism. In general, existentialism is a late nineteenth- and twentieth-century philosophical movement that assumes that, because there is no single definition of what it means to be human, each individual person is responsible for both defining and becoming a human on her own terms (thereby rejecting a notion that humans have an essence or teleology). Thus, existentialism is a philosophy that challenges people to be authentic to who they think they are without necessary reference to anything outside themselves.

Faust. Generally considered the greatest masterpiece of German literature, *Faust* is a two-part play by Johann Wolfgang von Goethe (first part, 1808; second part, 1832). Based on medieval legends of a sorcerer, Goethe's play transforms Faust into a modern figure who embodies a scholar's doubt and dissatisfaction with the world as offered to him. Convinced of the vanity of knowledge, Faust makes a pact with the devil (Mephistopheles) in order to gain more ability to manipulate the world in accordance with his desires.

Gloucester. "Gloucester" refers to Richard, Duke of Gloucester, who later became King Richard III of England. Richard had a short and tumultuous reign (1483–85), culminating in his death on the battlefield in what was to be the last of the Wars of the Roses. He is familiar to Kierkegaard through Shakespeare's play *Richard III*. In Shakespeare's portrayal, Richard is an amoral and tyrannical character.

Grundtvig, Nicolai (1783–1872). Grundtvig was an immense personality and a formative influence in several different fields in nineteenth-century Denmark. A scholar of Icelandic folk sagas and a passionate advocate for school reform, Grundtvig also had a dedicated following as a pastor. Two of his defining theological ideas were a commitment to oracular confession and the centrality of the Apostles' Creed (rather than Scripture) as the foundation of the church. Peter Christian Kierkegaard—a pastor and Søren's older brother—was a follower of Grundtvig.

Hegel, G. W. F. (1770–1831). Hegel was a German philosopher in the idealist tradition. Hegel's philosophy was an attempt to reconcile ancient and modern philosophy into a comprehensive system that could explain the history of the world in terms of the progressive movement of the Spirit. For Hegel, understanding the logic of history was the key to understanding the mind of God. Kierkegaard was highly critical of Hegel's "system," which he saw as an attempt to domesticate the transcendence of God.

Heiberg, J. L. (1791–1860). A leading figure of Danish Golden Age literature, Heiberg also made important contributions to the aesthetics and philosophy of his age. Heiberg played a key role in popularizing the philosophy of Hegel in Denmark, articulating a harmonious worldview in which philosophy, theology, and a generally refined culture combine in a glorious synthesis. Kierkegaard was, at best, ambivalent about Heiberg and the elite literary circle that surrounded him throughout his life.

Heraclitus (c. 535–c. 475 BCE). Heraclitus was a pre-Socratic Greek philosopher, known only through textual fragments, who has come to be identified with his embrace of the principle "everything flows" (*panta rhei*). According to Heraclitus, everything is constantly in flux (or everything is in a state of becoming, to put it in more technical philosophical language). This principle stands behind Heraclitus' famous maxim often translated as "you can never step into the same river twice."

ideological critique. Any set of ideas that grounds or supports a societal status quo is known as ideology. Ideological critique calls into question such beliefs, critically examining their legitimacy, accuracy, or internal coherence.

indirect communication. In brief, an attempt to communicate something through various means without stating it explicitly. Kierkegaard attempts this, for example, by constructing texts that might act as mirrors, thereby illuminating discrepancies or shortcomings in the reader that would be recognized upon reflection. Another way he attempts this is through creating texts that serve as signposts pointing beyond themselves. This practice also aligns with his conviction that he wrote without authority, as one who had not been ordained by the Danish Church.

irony. At a basic level, irony refers to a form of speech in which one does not mean what one says. The Romantics extended the meaning of irony to a form of life in which the internal subject does not correspond with the external actions it performs in the world. Irony in Kierkegaard's time, then, refers not just to a form of speech but to a form of life. Kierkegaard addresses this expansion of the significance of irony in his dissertation, *On the Concept of Irony*.

Jephthah. Jephthah was a judge in ancient Israel whose story is recounted in Judges 11–12. Jephthah frees Israel from the hands of the Ammonites but, in doing so, makes a vow to sacrifice the first thing he sees upon arriving home. The first thing he sees is his daughter, and he tragically fulfills his vow.

Kant, Immanuel (1724–1804). It could be said that modern critical philosophy as we know it begins with Kant. In his *Critique of Pure Reason* (1781), Kant posits a difference between objects as we experience them through our sensory capacities (phenomena) and objects as they are in themselves (noumena). Kant was also a major influence in moral theory—he formulated what is known as the categorical imperative, that one should act in such a way that one's action could be legislated for all people at all times. Furthermore, Kant wrote on the role of religion in *Religion within the Boundaries of Mere Reason*, arguing that it was a useful supplement to morality but should not be allowed to take pride of place over the latter.

Martensen, H. L. (1808–84). Martensen was a popular Danish philosopher and eventual bishop known for his Hegelian philosophy and defense of Christendom. Although Martensen was one of Kierkegaard's professors at

Copenhagen University, Kierkegaard strongly rejected Martensen's philosophy.

Moralität. In Hegel's *Elements of the Philosophy of Right* (1821), *Moralität* is the German term used to describe an ethics of individual rectitude, along the lines of Immanuel Kant's account of duty. Rather than one's place in society defining what is good for the moral agent, *Moralität* emphasized individual conviction and interior reflection.

Mother Teresa (1910–97). Mother Teresa was the founder of the Missionaries of Charity Sisters, a Catholic religious congregation devoted to serving the poor. Born in Albania, Mother Teresa moved to Calcutta, India, in 1958 to live and work among the poor in the slums. Much of her work was devoted to caring for abandoned and sick children, those with terminal illnesses, and the so-called untouchables of the Hindu caste system.

Mynster, Jakob Peter (1775–1854). Head of the Danish Church from 1834 until his death, Bishop Mynster was also Kierkegaard's boyhood pastor. Having gone through a crisis of faith early in his life, Mynster represented an urbane Christianity that managed to blend the philosophical proclivity of the elite with respect for popular piety. This synthesis of high culture with traditional religion proved compelling to many in Golden Age Denmark.

the negative (negation). The negative is a key element in Hegelian philosophy. According to Hegel, any development involves negation or opposition in regard to what precedes it. Rather than a simple logical relation, as it is traditionally thought of (p, -p), Hegel holds to the power of the negative in the production of progression. His understanding of the movement of sublation (*Aufhebung*) therefore entails a negation of the negative that takes it up in a new way.

Olsen, Regine (1822–1904). Kierkegaard and Olsen, in 1840, were engaged to be married. By October 1841, however, Kierkegaard had broken off the engagement. Kierkegaard wrote in his journals that he was unable to reconcile his vocation to be a critic of Christendom with his desire to marry. References to Regine can be found throughout Kierkegaard's journals and published books, even long after she married Johan Schlegel in 1847.

paradox. The paradox is closely connected with the absurd in Kierkegaard's thought. It refers to something that exists without being subject to objective reasoned analysis. As opposed to a strict contradiction (e.g., a square circle), a paradox contravenes opinions concerning what is possible in the world.

Pietists (Pietism). Generally thought to have begun with Philipp Jakob Spener (1635–1705), Pietism was a movement within the Lutheran tradition that emphasized passionate feeling and holy living above the rational analysis of doctrine. Groups of Pietists tended to form their own communities within the Lutheran church that held separate meetings.

propaedeutic. Etymologically, *propaedeutic* comes from two Greek words: *pro-*, meaning "before," and *paideutikos*, meaning "having to do with teaching." Propaedeutic is therefore the preliminary instruction that is necessary before the main subject is commenced.

Romantics (Romanticism). Romanticism is an intellectual and artistic movement that arose late in the eighteenth century largely in response to the Enlightenment. Opposed to the rationalism of Enlightenment philosophy, the Romantics employed categories that emphasized emotion, aesthetics, intuition, and creativity. Thus, Romanticism is marked by its drive to reach beyond what can be grasped by reason into the realm of the sublime—that which surpasses reason.

sectarianism. The most general definition of a sect is a coherent, identifiable group whose practices or beliefs are outside of the mainstream. Sectarianism refers to the tendency, attitude, or philosophy that leads to one group separating itself from broader society. In Kierkegaard's age, Pietists were one example of a sectarian group.

Sittlichkeit. In Hegel's *Elements of the Philosophy of Right*, *Sittlichkeit* is the German term used to refer to social ethics. In contrast to individual ethics, social ethics takes the welfare of society as a whole to be the defining aim of ethical action.

speculative (the speculative). Speculative philosophy is the attempt to deduce a metaphysical structure to the world apart from human experience. For Kierkegaard, Hegel's philosophy represents the speculative. Kierkegaard is adamant that theology cannot be speculative because Christianity is a lived existence that is rooted in an individual's direct experience with God.

Stoicism. A school of Greek philosophy begun in the third century BCE by Zeno of Citium, Stoicism had a vast influence on both philosophers and theologians. Its principal beliefs are twofold: (1) everything that happens is in line with *logos*, or the reason that governs the world; and (2) acceptance of the reasoned unfolding of events should lead to *apatheia*, or an emotional detachment from the immediate events one is experiencing.

temporality. Temporality is the everyday time and space that defines the world as humans ordinarily experience it, along with all the attendant cares and desires such time typically entails. In Kierkegaard, temporality is defined in sharp opposition to eternity.

Tobias and Sarah. The story of Tobias and Sarah can be found in the book of Tobit. Sarah has been married seven times, but each of her husbands has been killed on the wedding night by Sarah's tormentor, the demon Asmodaeus. Both Tobias and Sarah put their trust in God and go through with their marriage despite Sarah's past, and, in this case, protection from the demon is granted.

SUGGESTED READINGS

Barnett, Christopher B. *From Despair to Faith: The Spirituality of Søren Kierkegaard*. Minneapolis: Fortress, 2014.

Carlisle, Clare. *Kierkegaard's Fear and Trembling: A Reader's Guide*. London: Continuum, 2010.

Evans, C. Stephen. *Kierkegaard: An Introduction*. Cambridge: Cambridge University Press, 2009.

————. *Kierkegaard on Faith and the Self: Collected Essays*. Waco: Baylor University Press, 2006.

Ferreira, M. Jamie. *Kierkegaard*. Blackwell Great Minds 9. Malden, MA: Wiley-Blackwell, 2009.

Gouwens, David J. *Kierkegaard as Religious Thinker*. Cambridge: Cambridge University Press, 1996.

Green, Ronald M. "Enough Is Enough! *Fear and Trembling* Is *Not* about Ethics." *Journal of Religious Ethics* 21 (1993) 191–209.

Hannay, Alastair. *Kierkegaard: A Biography*. Cambridge: Cambridge University Press, 2001.

Kirmmse, Bruce H. *Kierkegaard in Golden Age Denmark*. Indiana Series in the Philosophy of Religion. Bloomington: Indiana University Press, 1990.

Lippitt, John. *Routledge Philosophy Guidebook to Kierkegaard and Fear and Trembling*. London: Routledge, 2003.

Lippitt, John, and George Pattison, eds. *The Oxford Handbook of Kierkegaard*. Oxford Handbooks. Oxford: Oxford University Press, 2013.

Lowrie, Walter. *A Short Life of Kierkegaard*. Princeton: Princeton University Press, 1942.

Pattison, George. *Kierkegaard and the Crisis of Faith: An Introduction to His Thought*. London: SPCK, 1997.

Rae, Murray. *Kierkegaard and Theology*. Philosophy and Theology. London: Continuum, 2010.

Walsh, Sylvia. *Kierkegaard: Thinking Christianly in an Existential Mode*. Christian Theology in Context. Oxford: Oxford University Press, 2009.

BIBLIOGRAPHY

Augustine, Saint. *Confessions*. Translated by Henry Chadwick. Oxford: Oxford University Press, 1991.

Barnett, Christopher B. *Kierkegaard, Pietism and Holiness*. Burlington, VT: Ashgate, 2011.

Bauckham, Richard. *James: Wisdom of James, Disciple of Jesus the Sage*. London: Routledge, 1999.

Camus, Albert. *The Myth of Sisyphus, and Other Essays*. Translated by Justin O'Brien. New York: Vintage, 1991.

Descartes, René. *Meditations on First Philosophy: With Selections from the Objections and Replies*. Edited and translated by John Cottingham. Rev. ed. Cambridge: Cambridge University Press, 1996.

Euripides. *Bacchae; Iphigenia at Aulis; Rhesus*. Edited and translated by David Kovacs. Cambridge: Harvard University Press, 2002.

Evans, C. Stephen. *Kierkegaard: An Introduction*. Cambridge: Cambridge University Press, 2009.

Hannay, Alastair. *Kierkegaard: A Biography*. Cambridge: Cambridge University Press, 2001.

Hegel, G. W. F. *Elements of the Philosophy of Right*. Edited by Allen W. Wood. Translated by H. B. Nisbet. Cambridge: Cambridge University Press, 1991.

———. *Lectures on the Philosophy of Religion*. Edited by P. C. Hodgson. Translated by R. F. Brown et al. 3 vols. Berkeley: University of California Press, 1984–87.

———. *Phenomenology of Spirit*. Translated by A. V. Miller. Oxford: Oxford University Press, 1977.

Kant, Immanuel. *Critique of Practical Reason*. Edited and translated by Mary Gregor. Cambridge: Cambridge University Press, 1997.

———. *Religion within the Bounds of Mere Reason and Other Writings*. Edited and translated by Allen Wood and George di Giovanni. Cambridge: Cambridge University Press, 1998.

Bibliography

Kierkegaard, Søren. *The Concept of Anxiety*. Edited and translated by Reidar Thomte in collaboration with Albert B. Anderson. Princeton: Princeton University Press, 1980.

———. *The Concept of Irony, with Continual Reference to Socrates*. Edited and translated by Howard V. Hong and Edna H. Hong. Princeton: Princeton University Press, 1989.

———. *Concluding Unscientific Postscript to Philosophical Fragments*. Edited and translated by Howard V. Hong and Edna H. Hong. Vol. 1. Princeton: Princeton University Press, 1992.

———. *Eighteen Upbuilding Discourses*. Edited and translated by Howard V. Hong and Edna H. Hong. Princeton: Princeton University Press, 1990.

———. *Either/Or*. Edited and translated by Howard V. Hong and Edna H. Hong. 2 vols. Princeton: Princeton University Press, 1987.

———. *Fear and Trembling*. Edited by C. Stephen Evans and Sylvia Walsh. Translated by Sylvia Walsh. Cambridge: Cambridge University Press, 2006.

———. *Fear and Trembling; Repetition*. Edited and translated by Howard V. Hong and Edna H. Hong. Princeton: Princeton University Press, 1983.

———. *For Self-Examination; Judge for Yourself!* Edited and translated by Howard V. Hong and Edna H. Hong. Princeton: Princeton University Press, 1991.

———. *The Moment and Late Writings*. Edited and translated by Howard V. Hong and Edna H. Hong. Princeton: Princeton University Press, 1998.

———. *Philosophical Fragments; Johannes Climacus*. Edited and translated by Howard V. Hong and Edna H. Hong. Princeton: Princeton University Press, 1985.

———. *The Point of View*. Edited and translated by Howard V. Hong and Edna H. Hong. Princeton: Princeton University Press, 1998.

———. *Practice in Christianity*. Edited and translated by Howard V. Hong and Edna H. Hong. Princeton: Princeton University Press, 1991.

———. *The Sickness unto Death*. Edited and translated by Howard V. Hong and Edna H. Hong. Princeton: Princeton University Press, 1983.

———. *Søren Kierkegaard's Journals and Papers*. Translated with notes by Howard V. Hong and Edna H. Hong; assisted by Gregor Malantschuk. 7 vols. Bloomington: Indiana University Press, 1967–78.

————. *Stages on Life's Way: Studies by Various Persons*. Edited and translated by Howard V. Hong and Edna H. Hong. Princeton: Princeton University Press, 1988.

————. *Without Authority*. Edited and translated by Howard V. Hong and Edna H. Hong. Princeton: Princeton University Press, 1997.

————. *Works of Love*. Edited and translated by Howard V. Hong and Edna H. Hong. Princeton: Princeton University Press, 1998.

Léon, Céline, and Sylvia Walsh, eds. *Feminist Interpretations of Søren Kierkegaard*. University Park: Pennsylvania State University Press, 1997.

Lippitt, John. *Humour and Irony in Kierkegaard's Thought*. New York: St. Martin's, 2000.

Plato. *Euthyphro; Apology; Crito; Phaedo; Phaedrus*. Translated by Harold North Fowler. Cambridge: Harvard University Press, 2001.

Rae, Murray. *Kierkegaard and Theology*. London: Continuum, 2010.

Roberts, Kyle. *Emerging Prophet: Kierkegaard and the Postmodern People of God*. Eugene, OR: Cascade, 2013.

Westphal, Merold. *Kierkegaard's Concept of Faith*. Grand Rapids: Eerdmans, 2014.

INDEX

Index

Made in the USA
Monee, IL
13 December 2019

18533698R00076